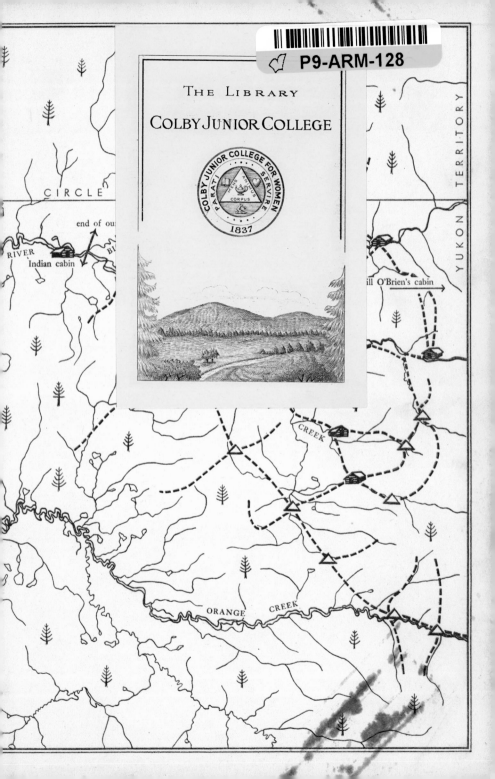

Born on Snowshoes

Born on

BY EVELYN BERGLUND SHORE

ILLUSTRATED WITH PHOTOGRAPHS AND

WITH DECORATIONS BY COURTNEY ALLEN

Snowshoes

HOUGHTON MIFFLIN COMPANY BOSTON

1954 · THE RIVERSIDE PRESS CAMBRIDGE

The Riverside Press
CAMBRIDGE · MASSACHUSETTS
PRINTED IN THE U.S.A.

Contents

List of Photographs

following page 148

Publisher's Note

EVELYN BERGLUND SHORE has written her own story, just as it happened. It is the story of incredible adventures and hardships in the northern wilderness, all of which she took as a matter of course and without any amazement.

When Evelyn was twelve her father, crippled by arthritis, gave up the weary struggle to support his family by fur trapping and retired to a hospital, leaving his wife and children to fend for themselves. In a situation where most women would have given up hope, Mrs. Berglund joined forces with John Roberts, an old trapper who had befriended the family, and, with only her three daughters to help them, they ran a trapline north of the Arctic Circle 280 miles beyond Fort Yukon. By courage, endurance, and literally endless work they made enough to support life. Nine years later, when Ernie Pyle met them on his visit to Alaska, they had paid back all the money they had borrowed and saved a little more, and the girls were almost grown. He wrote about them in his book, *Home Country:* "These girls grew up in the woods. . . . They knew no life but that of a trapper. They had never . . . seen a village with paved streets or brick buildings. . . . They didn't know much about men. They had never drunk or smoked, or danced or played cards. . . . But they had to shoot only once at a running moose, and they could freeze their feet without crying."

It was Pyle who urged Evelyn to keep a diary and write up her experiences. The diary was lost long ago but she needed no written record to help her to remember. It is all here — danger and tragedy, fun and excitement. As Ernie Pyle put it, "Nine years in the Far North, alone. Four women and an old man. Fighting, as we all do, for life."

Born on Snowshoes

I. A Northern Childhood

1. EARLIEST YEARS

I SUPPOSE that on the banks of American Creek in Alaska the hills were green with spruce and birch, and that wild flowers and berries spotted them and the valleys below. I suppose the small swift creek wound back and forth between the hills as though it couldn't make up its mind which side it liked best. That is the way an Alaskan creek usually acts; but though I was born there in a log cabin on July 30, 1917, I lived there only a short while, and remember little about it.

American Creek rose in the White Hills behind the little settlement of Eagle, and there was much mining activity along it. Dad and his brother, Oscar Berglund, owned mining claims there, and Mother in addition to her other chores cooked for the dozen or so men of the camp. When I was born, she and Dad had been in the North Country for five years, hoping to strike gold and make a stake. They had come in from Oregon in the spring of 1912.

Dad and Uncle Oscar had been in the north before that. Uncle Oscar had come in over Chilkoot Pass in '90, and had taken part in the Dawson gold rush. He had prospected on many creeks along the upper Yukon River. That was where Dad had joined him when he too got the gold fever.

After they returned to the States, Dad met my mother and married her, and they set up housekeeping in Oregon. But the call of the north was too much for Oscar. He had big dreams of striking it rich in the Klondike, and eventually he talked Dad and Mother into coming back with him to Dawson. They prospected there for a couple of years, and my eldest brother, George, was born there in 1913.

A year or so later they moved from the Yukon Territory down the Yukon River to Eagle, drifting and rowing in a small open boat by day and camping on gravel bars each night. When they reached Eagle they did not stop, but went up American Creek thirteen miles and staked out claims which they worked for the next five years. My sister Hazel was born there, then I, then my brother Charles.

This was a typical mining camp. There was a mess hall, a bunkhouse, and a barn for the one horse that Dad owned. We lived in a room adjoining the mess hall. The horse, a jack-of-all-trades, was used to bring supplies from Eagle, as a pack horse on hunting trips, and as a saddle pony.

Dad did a little trapping along with his mining, but neither the trapping nor the mining was very successful, and we moved on down the Yukon in the same rowboat and landed at a little town called Nation in the fall of 1919. Nation was much smaller than Eagle. Its total population was a half dozen old-timers and a dozen or so Indians.

Trying to make a living, Dad and Mother built a fish wheel and put it in the Yukon to catch salmon to be dried and sold. A fish wheel is something like a water wheel, having two large scoops fastened to a central axle. The scoops are turned by the current, one being in the water while the other is up. Fish are picked up in these scoops and slide down a board trough into a box at the end of the axle. The whole thing is kept afloat by a raft of logs on each side of the wheel, and is fastened to the bank by a heavy steel cable. Fish wheels are always placed along the high riverbanks where the water is deep and swift, for the swifter the water, the faster the wheel turns. Most wheels are put into the river about the middle of July when the king salmon start running in the upper Yukon, and are kept in until the ice starts to form. The king salmon run until the middle of August, but the red and dog salmon continue running until the freeze-up.

That winter of 1919, as soon as the fall hunting and the fishing were over, Dad started trapping. By then Uncle Oscar had left us and gone down the Yukon to Tanana. My younger sister Elsie was born on the seventeenth of February.

One of my few memories of our stay at Nation is of a potato patch we had in the summer of 1920. My brother George had slid off the roof of an old cabin and landed on a sleeping dog. Before the dog realized what had happened, he had jumped up and bit George on the head. This scared George, as well as Hazel and me, so badly that we ran pell-mell for home. The nearest way home was through the garden, and since George and Hazel were older, they ran faster and left me behind in it. I was only three years old, and if I had never seen a potato patch since I would say those plants were three feet tall. I couldn't see anything all around me but green bushes. Down the narrow rows straight ahead I ran and fell and crawled what seemed an endless way. When I finally made the cabin Mom was putting a bandage around George's head, and nobody paid any attention to me.

I got some attention out of the next experience, though. One morning in August I woke up and found Mom and Dad gone. I asked my brother where they were, and he said they were down at the fish wheel. Without any idea where that was, I started out to find them, dressed only in a white night-gown, and barefooted.

It was easier walking along the gravel bar than up among the tangled rosebushes on the bank, but at the end of the bar I came to a place where a grassy slough lay between me and the timbered bank. An old mammy bear and three cubs were fishing in the slough. The only animals I knew anything about were dogs; that's what I thought these were. I tried to catch the cubs, which ran around me as if I had been an old playmate. The old bear went on with her fishing, and paid no attention. The cubs ran after me and I ran after them, calling, "Come puppy, come puppy!" But I never could get quite close to them, and at last they ran to their mother, who stood up on her hind legs a moment, looked me over, and led them into the woods. I called to them but they would not come back.

Then I heard someone calling *me*, and there was my dad coming down the gravel bar. When I told him my puppies were lost, he walked back with me to where I had been play-ing and looked at the ground. "We don't want those pup-pies!" he said.

I have been told that I put my arms around Dad's neck and said, "Aren't you glad I found you, Papa?"

Telling the story later, Dad said that he did not see the bears, but he believed what I told him because the cub bear tracks were on top of mine in many places. Dad was a professional tracker. He had learned the trade in Australia. He had tracked me right from the house, and he said that I had walked two miles.

2. CABIN ON THE SHEENJACK

WE DIDN'T STAY at Nation long. Late in the fall of 1921 we were floating down the river again, planning to go on to join Uncle Oscar at Tanana, but the Yukon was running heavy slush ice, and we were frozen in at Fort Yukon. A number of people came down to the water's edge when we pulled in at the landing in front of a big log building. We climbed out of the boat shivering, and so stiff we could hardly walk, but we managed to jump up and down and yell "Goodie!" when a woman introduced herself to Mom and said, "Bring the children up to the house to get warm. You must be nearly frozen."

She was the wife of the wireless operator, and she made a pot of coffee for the grownups and one of cocoa for the children. We had our cocoa and cookies in one room with her two little girls while coffee was served to the older people in another. Those were almost the first little girls I had ever seen. When we had finished eating they brought in their dolls and toys to show us. Then their mother came in with a big bowl of walnuts, three hammers, and a plank longer than I was tall to crack them on. It still seems to me that that was one of the most exciting days of my childhood, and that there were more nuts there that day than I have ever seen since.

That winter Hazel and George got to go to school, and Hazel, though she was only five, finished the first grade. But next summer we were on the move again, this time up the Sheenjack River. Only little bits of memory remain about that trip, but I remember the time my mother tripped over the boat rope and spilled eight or ten big grayling into the river. She had cleaned them for supper and was on her way down to the river to wash them. The water was about two feet deep, and very clear, and when we saw the fish sinking we all thought our supper was gone. I guess it scared me enough so that I remember it. Dad rescued them and we had fish for supper after all.

We had no engine, and I can remember Mother pulling on the trackline with four dogs.

The trackline is a quarter-inch cotton rope three hundred feet long that is fastened to the bow of the boat. The dogs are harnessed and hitched to the end so that they can walk along the bar near the edge of the water. Mom walked a few feet behind the last dog to help the team pull and to clear the line from drift logs and roots. Dad stayed in the boat with a pole to keep it out in deep water and to help push in the swifter places. Sometimes he got out and waded in the water with hip boots on to guide the boat around shallow riffles.

About ninety miles upriver we stopped for a season of trapping. And the summer after that we moved three miles farther upriver and there on the Sheenjack Dad and Mother built the cabin that was to be our home for the next five years. They built it out of logs, but they went to a lot of trouble to whipsaw boards for a floor, and I remember how that went.

They built a scaffolding of logs about six feet off the ground so that they could pull a log up on it and block it so that it could not roll. Then they sawed a slab off each side, rolled the log onto a flat side and sawed the other two sides, and finally marked the squared log with chalk and sawed it into inch boards.

A whipsaw saws with the grain of the log. It has a big handle on the wide end that cannot be taken off, and a smaller one on the other end that is removable. Dad would stand on top and Mother on the ground under the log and they would saw up and down. To keep all the cuts even, they would saw about three feet in one, then Mother would take the handle off her end so that Dad could pull the saw up through and start another. When all the cuts were finished they had five or six nice boards. It took a long time, up and down, over and over, log after log, before we had a floor for our home.

That cabin on the Sheenjack was the place where we stayed longest while I was small, and I remember very clearly a lot of things that happened there. They were mixed things, good and bad, times when we were hard up, or out of food, or sick, times when we came close to getting in serious trouble with wild animals, times when it seemed that the river and the cabin and the country around us were the most exciting and wonderful place in the world.

Once we ran almost completely out of food, and Dad had to go back to town for supplies in midwinter. He tried to get a moose so that we would have something to eat while he was gone, but he had arthritis and couldn't get around as well as he might have, and he had no luck. When he left, all we had in the cupboard was one cup of rice, and we had to rustle our food or not eat. We rustled it by setting a lot of rabbit snares and shooting grouse with the .22. When Dad got back after about two weeks, we still had that cup of rice. Mom had been keeping it in case there would come a day when we didn't get any birds or rabbits, but she hadn't told us children that. We all thought we were saving it for Dad's return. It never occurred to us that he would have food with him when he came back.

The next summer we didn't go to town at all. On the evening of July 19 Mother told us to go to bed and get to sleep as soon as we could, and in the morning she would let us all look at the new baby who was going to come that night. We did, and next morning ran over to her bed. The baby was a tiny little thing, not much larger than my sister's big doll. Mother told us it was a little boy, and we were all pleased because now we were even, three boys and three girls. Mother stayed in bed all day. We wondered why, but she said she had to stay close to the new baby.

About three o'clock that afternoon three-year-old Elsie began to cry and say that she was sick. When we found her temperature was 102°, we put her to bed. Next day I didn't feel well. I was cold, though it was eighty above zero, and when I crawled into a feather sleeping bag to get warm I fell asleep. Sometime later I was awakened by Dad, saying, "What are you doing in that feather robe on a hot day like this? Your face is all red."

I said, "I was cold, and I'm still cold."

He took my temperature and sent me to bed.

Later that afternoon my oldest brother followed me. Hazel and Charley bragged that they were too tough to get sick, but by the third day they were in bed, too. That made five of us, and Mother with a new baby. The baby was the only one who didn't get sick, for that matter, because Mother and Dad both came down. Mother tried to doctor us with castor oil, custards, and rice water, but after a week we were all as sick as when we had gone to bed. That was when Mother told Dad to get in the canoe and go to town for a doctor.

Dad was a little better, though he wasn't well. The nearest doctor was in Fort Yukon, forty-three miles down the Sheenjack and Porcupine Rivers and a couple of miles up the Yukon from the mouth of the Porcupine. Dad went for him the next day and came back with him nine days later. By that time we were all feeling better, and so he turned around and took the doctor back and was gone another ten days.

We were able to get up a little while each day, but not able to do much. It helped a lot when two men stopped on their way down the river and stayed for four days, cutting wood and packing water. They even did a little cooking, and when they left us we had a nice stack of stovewood.

We were down there where they had been chopping, picking up chips to save the woodpile because we didn't know when Dad would be back, when Mother picked up her rifle and said, "I think I saw a porcupine below the bank. Keep quiet."

We all stayed still while she went over to the edge. After a minute she raised the gun and fired. We heard a thud and saw the willows shaking, but Mom said, "Stay back while I go down and look."

In a couple of minutes she called to us to come down and

see the big black bear she had shot. George and Hazel ran home and brought an ax and butcher knife and we skinned and butchered the bear and packed him home in small pieces. By the time we had finished we were all weak and tired out. We asked Mother if we could have a steak. She said she was afraid it was too fresh and that we weren't strong enough yet to be eating bear steak, but we all begged and promised to take an extra dose of castor oil if we got sick. So she fried a steak for each of us, and we didn't get sick!

Nearly five years later, Mom was talking to a doctor on the steamboat. She told him our symptoms and he said it was probably intestinal flu and that she was very lucky to have saved us.

We got into enough trouble to keep things lively, and though Dad's bark was worse than his bite we got our share of punishment. We christened the cabin, before it was even quite finished, in a way that hadn't been planned.

Late in September, when the floor was only about half laid, we moved in. On this day there was a cold wind blowing, and Mom told us to stay home and do the dishes while she and Dad went over and sawed lumber for the floor. Ten minutes later we looked across the lake drainage back of the house and saw Dad standing in his place on top of the saw log.

Our orders were forgotten, and we started a game. George and I were bears, while Hazel and Charley were hunters. They each got a kindling stick for a gun and George and I went out behind the house, waited for a couple of minutes, and came back on our hands and feet toward the big single-paned glass window, the only one of its kind in the house.

The others all had six small panes. As George reached the house he rose up on his legs and let out an awful growl. Charley, who was standing inside by the pan of dishes, was only four years old; everything was very real to him. First he threw the kindling stick at George but it only bounded off the glass. Then George put both hands up beside his head like ears and snarled and growled as loud as he could.

Charley screamed and grabbed the egg beater off the dishpan and threw it with all his might. George and I fell flat on the ground when we saw it coming. We heard a chilling shattering and glass sprayed all over us. When we jumped to our feet Charley was still screaming and Hazel was holding his wrists to keep him from throwing the flatiron he clutched in his hand. His face was as white as paper. He kept screaming, "He's a bear, Hazel, run!"

George and I came in and told him we weren't bears any more, but he still shook like a leaf in a wind. To quiet him down, George suggested a pillow fight. The house was getting cold from the open window, so we piled the cookstove full of wood. Hazel threw a pillow at me, missed, grabbed another, and the fight was on.

Sometime later Elsie, who was the baby then, started to cough. "What's burning?" George said. We turned and looked.

The ceiling was completely blotted out by thick white smoke which poured through the window and the open door. On the stove lay a pillow with a red fringe of sparks rising around it, and a column of smoke such as I have never seen since going up from the feathers on the red-hot stove lids.

George put his hands to his head with a moan, grabbed the

pillow by one corner, and ran for the door, leaving a trail of black, crisp, half-burned feathers across the floor. As soon as the pillow hit the ground outside the cover and slip burst into flames. The wind, blowing from the house toward the saw pit, carried the smoke with it, and through the willows Mom and Dad saw the smoke and flames and imagined the worst. When Dad arrived on the run a few moments later we were all so busy trying to clean up the mess of overturned chairs, boxes, pots and pans that we never heard a thing until he said, "What the hell's going on here?"

We jumped to attention and said as one, "Papa, we won't do it again!"

"I'll bet you won't," he said.

He made us pick up with our fingers every feather that George had spilled. The window he plugged with a big piece of brown cardboard from a packing box, but the smell of burned feathers stayed in the house for a long time.

We liked to climb trees, and we mastered every one we could find but one tall cottonwood. How we longed to climb that tree, but there was not a single branch for fifteen feet, and the trunk was too big for shinnying up. Every time we passed it we looked longingly at it, until at last George got an idea: he thought of some eight-inch spikes that Dad had.

The idea worked fine. Within a half hour all four of us older ones had gone up the spike footholds and were high in the top of the cottonwood. It was wonderful to be up there above the tops of the shorter trees. We could see far out over the lakes and rivers and see grass flats and sloughs that we hadn't even known were there. We even saw a black bear on the edge of a nearby lake, pretty there in the bright green grass.

When Mom whoo-whooed at us we didn't answer from the treetop, but waited until we had climbed down. George grabbed the hammer and hid it under his clothes when we got near the house. That evening we were really good, and went to bed when we were told. But the next day we were up the tree again.

It was September, and Dad had been away on a hunting trip. But now he came home, and almost the first thing he wanted was his spikes. We helped him look through everything in the shed, but we couldn't find them. Privately we tried to pull them out of the tree, but they were in to stay. And anyway we weren't too sorry. As long as they were there we could spend part of every day up the cottonwood.

About a week later Dad went hunting again, upriver. Our tree was downriver from the cabin, and we had no worries as we swung and swayed and yelled in the branches. But he didn't come home the way he had gone, for suddenly we heard him say, "What in hell are you kids doing up that tree?" And then he came closer and saw his spikes. "All right," he said. "Get down and go straight home. I'll see you there."

We all said, "But papa . . ."

"Forget the 'buts.' I'll see you later."

I told George that I would say I took the spikes; spankings always seemed to hurt George worse than they did me. But we all got our whippings anyway, and then Dad told us to go down and pull out the spikes. We told him we already had tried. He came down with us and tried himself, but with no better luck. We were beginning to think we would be able to go on climbing the tree when he looked back over his shoulder once more and then went and drove in to their heads all the spikes he could reach. "Maybe that'll stop you," he said. "Don't you realize you could kill yourselves?"

It didn't quite stop us, for we took a ladder down and climbed the tree whenever we were sure Dad wasn't around to see us. Only two at a time climbed while the other two stood watch on the ground.

One day while Hazel and George were in the tree, Charley and I went over to the bridge, a little farther out on the trail, in case Dad might come home that way again. With a rabbit snare on the end of a pole we fished roots out of the nearly dry creek that drained the lake. The banks of this natural drainage ditch were ten feet high, and there were lots of dead roots below the bridge Dad had built. We had heard Dad speak of "deadoaks," and imagined they were some fierce animal; we named these things deadoaks and fished them out until we had the bridge jammed with them. No one could get across. We kept on working with them, beating them on what we called their heads, until we looked up and saw Dad coming.

Charley yelled in what he meant to be a happy and excited voice, "Papa's coming!"

The tree climbers came down in a hurry and ran for home with the ladder while Charley and I worked like beavers tearing down our bridge block, explaining all the time that we hadn't known Dad was coming home that way or we never would have fished out deadoaks that day. Dad told us that if we ever jammed up the bridge again we would be dealt with as we should be.

We did jam it up many times after that, and we wore striped pants for our trouble. To us, deadoaks were very exciting things to catch. It was years before I knew that a deadoak was really just a dead oak tree.

Most of our games and sports were like that — we had to invent them or make the equipment. But I don't think anyone ever had more fun than we did, especially when winter closed in.

Dad made us a merry-go-round on a small lake about a city block from the house. Just before the ice formed he cut a long post about six inches in diameter and took it out and drove it into the lake bottom, as near the middle as he could. When the ice froze around it, the post was held very solid. Then he drove a half-inch iron bar down into the center of the post, leaving about five inches of iron sticking above the top, and took a spruce pole about thirty feet long and bored a hole through it about ten feet from the big end. Through this hole he fitted the iron bar, and after that he made a little one-runner sled that he fastened to the long end of the pole. One child rode the sled while three or four others powered the merry-go-round from the short end of the pole. We put out a lot of work shoveling snow and sweeping the track for the merry-go-round until the snow finally became too deep, generally around the last of January when the wind would drift it in faster than we could clear it out.

When that happened we dug into the high ring of solid snow and made snow houses with connecting tunnels. By the time we were finished we each had two or three snow houses, all connected, and we could go clear around the merry-go-round circle without ever coming out.

Sometimes we went down to the river where the wind had crusted the snow, and sawed out blocks with a handsaw sneaked from Dad's toolbox. With a small stick we would outline a dog, doll, dish, or whatever we wanted to make, and then go round and round the outline until the outer pieces fell off and the sculpture was completed. These toys were very breakable and had to be handled with the greatest care. Often when they were finished and were being carefully taken to the snow house they were broken to bits if their toter made a misstep or fell with them.

It always seemed to us that we no sooner got our snow houses finished and furnished than it was spring and the sun started melting them away, and we had to stand around and watch all our hard work vanish. Each spring Dad helped us take the merry-go-round down and cache it on the edge of the lake; each fall we put it up again.

There was no limit to what we would do for some good coasting on our little sled and toboggan. Once on the slough bank we shoveled snow for three days to level out the bumps and make a good slide. And then when it was finished it was too short to suit us.

But the bank in front of our house was about thirty feet high, and Dad had shoveled a trail down it at an angle. This made a straight slide of more than sixty feet, and it was our favorite coasting place. One day when Dad was packing water up from the water hole chopped in the river ice, he splashed some on the trail about halfway up. When our sled hit this icy spot it fairly leaped, and that gave us an idea. If the trail were all glaciered we could go much faster.

It was late afternoon, but we got four cans and set to work packing water up from the water hole and pouring it on the trail, starting at the top and working down until the hill was well soaked. Then we climbed straight up the bank, in order not to make tracks in the wet snow, and went into the house.

We thought only of the fun we would have next day until Mom said, "George, we need more water tonight. One can will do."

Dad dropped his book into his lap and asked, "Are both cans empty?"

She said they were. He got up and took the two cans and the yoke, saying it was just as easy to carry two with the yoke as to carry one by hand. When he started out of the house we looked at each other, but said nothing. In about two minutes Dad returned. One of the five gallon cans was smashed flat. He took another from the shed and started for the water hole again, and a second time he returned. We heard him throw the yoke down, and he called to Mom. "Maud, send one of the kids out with the flashlight. I've fallen twice and smashed two cans. I'll have to try it with one can and a light."

George took the flashlight out, and I followed him. Dad shone the light on the trail. He said, "Who spilled water all over this?"

We both said, "I don't know."

He looked farther down the trail. "Damn those kids!" he said, and went back to the house and told Mom what he had seen. Then he said, "You kids get busy and get your Mama some water!"

We got the can and took the little toboggan and tied a long rope to it. George got into it with the water can and we let him down to the river. When he had filled the can, we pulled it and the toboggan back up, while he climbed straight up the bank as we had done before.

As soon as we got the water into the house Dad said, "Now get to bed." We did, without any delay. Dad had hurt his hip and he saw nothing funny about the whole thing. The next day he told us he wanted that trail put into shape and he didn't want any delay about it. We cut steps all the way down, but it was still slick, and so he made us go to where we emptied the ashes from the stove and scatter ashes all over the icy trail. It took us nearly all day to fix it so we could walk up and down safely. We never did get a chance to scoot down with our sled, and we never glaciered it again.

Since we lived forty-three miles from Fort Yukon and there was no one living within twenty miles of us on either side, we never had much company, but when we did it was a big event. The man who trapped the line above us, Jim Carroll, had a native wife and three or four children, but we never saw them. We saw Jim only because he sometimes came past on his way to town for supplies, and when he passed he generally left us a chunk of moose meat. We always had plenty of snowshoe rabbits, but they got pretty tiresome, and those fat moose steaks were a treat. And when Jim stayed overnight, as he often did, we kids really enjoyed ourselves. Every ordinary morning, winter and summer, we had mush and hotcakes for breakfast, but when Jim was there we skipped the mush and had moose steak and hotcakes. Jim's trips to town were actually among the most important events in our young lives, for he nearly always brought us out a big bag of candy and sometimes a dozen or so packages of gum.

December was a big month for us, for Hazel's birthday was the eighteenth, George's the twenty-second, and Charley's the twenty-third. Then came Christmas. But sometimes there wasn't much we could do about it. I especially remember the Christmas of 1926, when I was nine.

On Christmas Eve the sky was cloudy and a cold wind was blowing. Outside the thermometer said twenty below zero. Mother told us to go to bed and get a good night's sleep, because tomorrow would be Christmas, and when we asked if we were going to have a tree, even though we had no presents to open, she said she thought Dad had a tree to put up, but now to go to bed.

Christmas morning came, dark and cloudy; not even a star peeped through the windows. I opened my eyes once, then closed them and cuddled down closer to my sister. What was there to get up for? It was cold and dreary and we wouldn't have anything nice or special for Christmas. I didn't even want to get up a half hour later when I heard Mother clattering the pans as she started to cook breakfast. Our cabin had only one room, but I didn't even care to open my eyes and look at her. I didn't care to see the dark shadows that the coal-oil lamp made. They scared me, reminding me of the ghost stories Dad often told us after we had turned in for the night.

I heard Mother putting dishes on the table, and then I heard her say, "George, we're ready," and heard the striking of a match.

"Get up, kids!" she called. "Breakfast's ready."

We wiggled and groaned. "Hurry," she said. "Dress fast."

Then we got up and looked around, and the cabin was filled with the red glow of candlelight and in the middle of the room stood the prettiest Christmas tree I had ever seen. The silver and gold stars, the crescents and the bells that we had been making from cardboard and from the tinfoil of tea packages and Dad's tobacco cans all through the fall were hanging on it, and gold tinsel and colored-paper chains were thrown over the branches.

Each long branch was tipped with a red, blue, green, or yellow candleholder with a little candle of another color in it. The house was lighted only by the tiny candles. Nearer the trunk of the tree were hanging little pink paper baskets. We looked: raisins. There were little packages wrapped in red or green crepe paper. Each contained a candied fig. At the foot of the tree lay six large packages, all long and looking very much alike except that each had the name of a different one of us on it.

I don't know how I got into my clothes; I do know I didn't want to eat my breakfast. When Mother told us we could open our packages we just stood and looked until she put them in our arms. "Go ahead, open them. When you're ready, there are a little pink basket and three little packages for each of you on the tree. You may take them off yourselves."

Each package contained a big rag doll. Mine had a deep purple silk dress. It was so pretty that I've forgotten the dresses the other two girl dolls had on. The boys' dolls wore little shirts and overalls. Mother had made the six dolls and dressed them at night, after we were asleep. They were of canvas, stuffed with moose hair, their faces embroidered with colored yarns, and each had yarn hair.

3. BERRYPICKING AND THE BRUSH MAN

WHERE we lived on the Sheenjack River the only berries were high-bush cranberries. They were good solely for jelly, and we seldom got many because when we came out from town to the trapline about the middle of September the berries were too ripe to jell. But the Indians around Fort Yukon, earlier in the season, got plenty of low-bush cranberries, and one day an old Indian woman told Mom she would show her a patch. Her name was Old Belle. She said, "You get ready nine in the morning, then we go. You take grub. We be gone all day."

Mom said, "You come to my house. I'll be ready. I'll make lunch for you too."

Belle shook her head. "No, me no eat white man grub, me take little dry meat and little water, that plenty."

"Well, don't forget to stop for us."

"Oh, me no forget."

Belle lived about fifty yards from the cabin where we stayed in Fort Yukon, and had to go by on her way to the woods. But next morning Mom was ready on time, and no Belle. She waited until nine-thirty and then sent Hazel to see what Belle was doing. Belle had left at eight o'clock. Mom was really angry, because she wanted some berries. She slammed the lunch and the empty pails on the table and said, "No berrypicking today. I could break that old squaw's neck."

Dad got up and told us to take care of the house. "Your mother and I are going to find out where Belle gets her berries."

"Are you going to try tracking her to the patch?" Mom asked.

"You'll be picking beside her by noon."

Mom and Dad tracked them two miles and finally came upon Belle and her party busy picking. Dad slipped aside with a wink and Mom went ahead, calling as she neared the patch, "Hello, Belle, how are the berries?"

Belle jumped.

"How you find us?"

Mom pointed to Belle's feet, but Belle put out both hands as if to shove her away. "No, no! Me wear moccasin, me no make track. You medicine woman. You smell all same dog smell."

Dad smiled to himself and crumbled a handful of tobacco to fill his pipe. They picked beside Belle and her party all afternoon, and she took them to the best patches she knew about. The old woman was really scared, and she never ran away from us again. We spent a good many days after that wandering through the woods from one patch to another. Belle often gave me a big hunk of dried meat out of her lunch sack, saying, "Dry meat make strong kid, you be big strong girl some day."

But sometimes Belle didn't feel like going, and we went without her. On one of these days Mom and a part-Indian girl and I left the wood road about noon and sat down in a small berry patch to eat lunch. Afterward we went along picking berries. Before long we came to a pile of newspapers. Our first thought was that someone else was out picking, but when we looked at the papers we found they were the ones our own lunch had been wrapped in. Mom said, "Well, let's go on out to the road. There aren't any more berries here anyway."

When we had walked in what we thought the direction of the road for a while we came upon the same lunch papers. And after we had tried again, getting more confused, we tried to go back to the lunch place but couldn't find it. The sky filled with clouds, and by midafternoon it was raining, and we were soaked. The bushes were dripping, and they brushed across our faces until water ran from our chins. Everything was wet and cold. The dark gray sky gave no sign of where the sun might be.

About eight o'clock we came to a "niggerhead flat" with a tall dead spruce in the middle of it. Niggerheads are found in fairly open country. I have no idea how they came by that name. They are grass clumps in which the grass grows from a rotten stump. The grass is strong and hairlike, growing from the middle of the clump and hanging down from a foot to as much as three feet. When dead it is light brown, but it never falls off, just hangs, year after year, each season adding to the outside diameter of the clump. In summer there is water between the clumps in some places, and this makes an ideal breeding ground for mosquitoes and gnats. Most niggerhead flats in the mountainous country contain large patches of blueberries. This one didn't have any blueberries, but it had plenty of mosquitoes.

The dead spruce had three blazes on it, with arrows pointing. One said, "To cabin," another "To trail," but the writing was so old that we could not tell which sign went with which arrow. As we stood debating whether to set the spruce on fire as a signal of distress or to try finding our way home, we saw a lake. The Indian girl said the only lake she knew about was on the Sucker River wood road. We decided to go around the lake and if we didn't find the trail to come back and set the tree on fire.

Just before we came to the lake I saw a break in the clouds and through it a pink glow. I said, "Mom, I see where the sun is."

She said, "Well, we're going the right direction, anyhow."

We circled the lake and as we neared the other end we came to a wide road leading straight into the water. This was the winter wood road. By following it we eventually got back to Fort Yukon at nine-thirty that night.

Still, being lost in the woods is no fun. The Indians like it even less than we did, mainly because they are afraid of the Brush Man.

I have heard many stories of the Brush Man, and many explanations of what he is. One old woman told us the Indian Brush Man is the same as the white man's Devil, and that the only way to keep him away is to carry a prayer book. For some strange reason the Brush Man is supposed never to bother a white person. The Indians believe in him completely, though. They told us about a very pretty little halfbreed girl who was stolen away while a party was out picking cranberries. They had laid the two- or three-year-old baby down under a tree while they picked, and when they went to get her she was not there. Jumping to the conclusion that the Brush Man had stolen her, they hurried into town and told everyone what had happened. They also went to church and prayed for the return of the little girl, and after that they went out to search for her, each carrying his prayer book. Going to the place where they had been picking berries, they found the child fast asleep under the same tree where they had left her. Skeptical white people thought the child had been there all the time, and that the Indians had simply mistaken the tree they had put her under, but the Indians were all sure the Brush Man had taken her and then been scared by the prayers into putting her back.

Another woman once gave me an explanation of the origin

of the Brush Man. She said that in the old days before the white men came the Indians followed the game from place to place. When they killed a moose or caribou they camped by the carcass until it was entirely eaten. Then they moved on until they killed another. They never had anything to eat except what they killed from day to day.

They traveled in large groups, the young men doing the hunting, the old men making snowshoes and bows and arrows, fixing toboggans, and so on, while the women took care of the children and did the tanning and sewing and cooking. Their way of living was very hard, and when game was scarce whole villages might be close to starving. This was where the Brush Man got his start. It seems that there was a tribal law that no man should ever eat another man. They ate their dogs, but when a member of any village died they put him in a crude coffin and hung him high in a tree. But at starving times some man or woman might eat one of the dead. When this was found out, the offender was driven away and never allowed to return. The outcast roamed the woods until he starved. Occasionally a strong man would not die, but instead became a dangerous enemy to the rest of the group, turning cannibal and stealing away children to eat, and even killing men who were hunting alone. Thus the Brush Man could have started out as a reality, and a very menacing one.

4. MUSKRATS, A BEAR, AND A MOOSE

ALMOST FROM the time we could walk, all of us were trappers. On the Sheenjack we all ran trap and snare lines, and though they were like a game to us, they were not entirely play. On the rabbit snare lines that Mother helped us run, we caught over three hundred rabbits one winter, and that many rabbits will go a long way to providing a winter's meat supply. Along about the first of October, when the lakes and rivers were beginning to freeze over and the first snow covered the ground, we made snares out of No. 2 picture wire and set out many lines of them. Most of our rabbit-snaring was done in the next month, before the trapping season opened.

Once it got really cold, we put out our traps just like Dad. We caught several mink, a couple of lynx, and a good many ermine and muskrat in those years, and we had our share of trapper's excitement. After all, the animals didn't know we were just playing.

One day George and I went out with the dogteam to look at some mink traps we had set about three miles from home. George was thirteen, I was nine. About two miles out, near the end of a long lake, the dogs started to run, and we couldn't stop them. Then we heard a wolf howl, and we kept on hearing him howl as we got closer. Finally the dogs got scared and lay down, so that George had to run up to the leader and lead him back to turn the team toward home. By that time he could hardly keep them from bolting back in the direction we had come from.

"Get in and hang on!" he yelled to me, and let the leader go. As the toboggan went past him he threw himself across it; I grabbed him and helped him in. The dogs were loping with their tails down and their ears lying flat on their necks. When we looked back to see if we could see what they were running from, we saw four big gray wolves, one sniffing our trail where we had turned back, the others coming up toward him.

That was when we really wanted the dogs to run. Going through bushes, we had to lie flat on the toboggan to keep from getting whipped off, and we never stopped running until we were home.

Those winter traplines were a little hard for us, young as we were, but we were more help with the muskrats in the spring. "Ratting" started about the first of March. Mom would take a couple of us, leaving the other two at home to look after the baby, and set out muskrat traps in the lakes nearest the house. Usually she trapped about six lakes, using two hundred traps. Dad trapped farther from home, putting out about the same number. Generally we averaged about fifteen hundred muskrats a year. In our best year we got twenty-eight hundred, and in the worst, our last, eight hundred. Mother always trapped muskrats until the ice went out, and after that, until the season closed on June 1, she shot them.

Late in the spring, when the mating season started, the rats were unfit to eat, but in the early part of the season they tasted awfully good after a winter of rabbit. Mom skinned them, soaked them in salt water overnight, and roasted them. Often she stuffed them with sage dressing and served them with thick brown gravy, taking as much care over them as you would take over a Thanksgiving turkey. Sometimes we had rice with them, or if we were lucky, mashed potatoes, and sometimes we finished off with cookies or cinnamon rolls, bread pudding, or pie or cake.

We loved to go hunting the muskrats after the ice thawed around the margins of the lakes and the pasqueflowers were blooming where the snow was off the ground. From the first of April on we kept a bouquet of pussywillows on the stand near where Mother sat with her sewing. As soon as the pussywillows were past, pasqueflowers took their place. I still remember going out to Loon Lake, a quarter mile from home, and picking all the beautiful lavender flowers we could carry home. Often we saw black bears; whenever we did we ran for home as fast as we could go.

One day in early spring Dad took his shotgun and canoe to go shooting rats over on Loon Lake. We all wanted to go. Finally he said, "Oh, well, come along and scare everything away. There are probably no rats out yet anyway."

On Loon Lake the pasqueflowers were blooming in great numbers, though the ice was not yet thawed enough to let us use the canoe. Each of us four children picked a big bunch of the pale purple flowers for Mom while Dad walked around the edge of the lake and shot a half-dozen muskrats that ventured out. Then we all walked back to the canoe, where Dad told us to stay while he went to see how the ice was thawing in the next lake.

As soon as he was out of sight we decided to hide and scare him when he came back. We crawled under the canoe and let it down on top of us. As we hid there, keeping as still as we could, hardly breathing, we heard footsteps coming toward us, right up to the canoe, touching it. Any minute we expected Dad to lift the canoe off us, but the steps went away again. We were all very quiet, and then George whispered, "Don't anybody move. That wasn't Papa. I think it was a bear."

We were too scared to breathe. We could hear our own hearts beating. Then footsteps again, and finally Dad's voice, "Now where did those darn kids go?"

We yelled, "Right here, Papa! Under the canoe. Get us out quick!"

He lifted the canoe and we scrambled out panting and gasping. Dad said, "Why did you go under there? You look half-smothered."

"We wanted to scare you," we said. "But something big walked up and bit the canoe. We didn't move, so he went away."

Dad looked all around at the ground, and said, "There are bear tracks here, all right. Let's see where he bit the canoe."

But all he could find was a wet swipe six inches long across the bottom. Dad looked at it for a few moments, and then said, "Once in a while you kids do show a little sense. If you'd tried to come out from under there while the bear was here you'd probably have been killed."

Dad's arthritis was often so bad that he couldn't go out and hunt, and we never had enough moose meat. But it always seemed that if he did go hunting, and we didn't have a rifle around the house, something came right up to us. One evening when Dad was away overnight a big bear walked through the yard between the house and the dog kennels. Another time the dogs started barking about four o'clock in the morning, when it was still too dark to see anything. Through the window we could just make out a big dark hulk moving around the yard and charging the dogs every time one stuck his head out of a kennel. The dogs made so much noise that sleep was out of the question. We sat up and watched until it got light enough to see that we were being visited by a big bull moose. He kept pawing the ground and making rushes at the dogs.

A few dishtowels and a pink nightgown were hanging on the clothesline stretched from the corner of the house to the cache. Suddenly a gust of wind set them flapping, and the moose saw them. With a wild snort he charged. The house shook as his horns clashed into the wire line and broke it loose. When we rushed to the window to see better he was standing with the towels and nightgown and line wrapped around his horns, and pawing and shaking his head to get free.

After a minute he shook off the wire and the dishtowels, but he still wore the pink nightgown. Mom had lighted a coal-oil lamp and set it in the window so we could see him better. We roared with laughter at him, and the noise and light attracted his attention. With another snort he charged straight for the window.

"Get back, kids!" Mom yelled. She rolled us away just as he hit the house as if he would knock it down. Then the dogs all came rushing out to bark, and he turned to charge them, and Mom blew out the light quickly.

"How long will he stay, Mom?" Hazel said.

Mom said she didn't know, but she hoped until Dad got home.

As it grew lighter the dogs stopped barking, and about nine o'clock the moose and the nightie walked off into the woods and did not return. Dad came home about ten-thirty and took out on his track, but he never caught up with him. Once the moose decided to move on, he never stopped. Maybe he was ashamed of the pink nightgown he was wearing.

5. SUMMER OF 1927

THAT WAS THE WAY our childhood went on the Sheenjack, and it went that way until the summer of 1927, a summer I will never forget.

A few weeks after we brought our furs out to Fort Yukon, Dad went into the hospital for treatment of his arthritis. Mother worked, doing housework for the neighbors and taking in washing to do at home. Because we couldn't afford to buy firewood, we children gathered wood from the forest back of town.

About three o'clock in the afternoon on June 14 Dad came home from the hospital. The treatments hadn't done him any good, and we couldn't afford to keep them up. That evening Hazel and I were doing the dishes and George and Charley were down at the river having what they called a "dragon fight," playing that the dragonflies were some kind of dragons that chased them. Dad had asked them to bring the oars back from the boat when they came up.

A half hour after we had finished with the dishes, Mother said, "Call the boys in, Evelyn."

I called and called, but got no answer. "Well, then," Mother said, "go down and tell them to come right home."

Down on the riverbank I could find no sign of them. Along the waterfront clear to the steamboat landing in front of the Northern Commercial Store I went calling. Then I came home by the road through town, asking all I met if they had seen the boys. No one had.

When I got home and told Mother I could not find the boys, she started out to find them herself.

She had not found them by morning. The whole town, turning out to help, had not found them when ten days had passed. On that day a hard thunderstorm came up, and all night the lightning flashed and thunder rolled. At midnight an old Indian woman came to the door and told us that Charley's body had been found in the Yukon.

They found George a little later, and they had a double funeral. Mother would not let us go. Dad, almost helpless, was then at the hot springs at Circle. She left us to take care of the house and she went to the funeral alone.

That fall we did not go back on the Sheenjack, for Dad was too crippled to do anything. He was still in the hospital when Mom sent up a launch to get our things down to town, and he stayed in the hospital most of the time after that. Mom took in washing and did odd jobs around town, and we got a little help from the Red Cross and made it through the winter. We went to school — the first time for Elsie and me, the last time for any of us. I remember that winter for the hard times, and the school, and the plane that brought the first air mail from Fairbanks to Fort Yukon. When it landed on the ice of the Yukon River in front of our house it seemed to me it came from another world.

II. Up the Salmon River

1. A NEW START

EVERYBODY LIKED John Roberts, mainly because he was always ready to help out anyone in trouble. He was a little stooped man of sixty, one shoulder crooked from a logging accident years before, his face and head bushy with red hair and whiskers. He had a trapline on the Salmon Fork of Black River, two hundred and eighty miles by water, one hundred twenty five by airline from Fort Yukon. When he went out in the summer he took his supplies and outfit on a thirty-four-foot boat, powered with a 15-30 Universal inboard engine, and towing a thirty-foot poling boat. He had a good trapline, a good outfit, and a big heart. When he got to know us and saw how crippled Dad was with arthritis, and heard how we had had to sell our trapline on the Sheenjack for two hundred dollars to get us through the winter, he invited us to go out that year with him. Then he loaned Dad a thousand dollars to buy a winter's food supply, and he bought lumber for a scow and helped Dad build it.

Loading took us all one day. We had to put cases of canned goods and sacks of flour on the floor of the boat and sugar and paper cartons and perishables on top, so that nothing would be damaged if the scow sprang a bad leak. Flour is resistant to water as long as it isn't mixed about. If a wet sack is lifted out carefully and allowed to dry, a crust forms around the wet part and protects the inside.

Pete Nelson and Bill O'Brien, two other trappers, were going with us that summer of 1928. We were five boats in all, with nine people and a good many dogs. Bill's outfit was loaded in the front of our scow, just behind Pete's. John's poling boat was loaded with dry fish for dog feed and seven dogs. Bill's poling boat held his camp outfit and four dogs. Pete had no dogs, but his poling boat was full of his camp equipment. That left the power boat for our camp outfit, Mother, and us kids.

On each side of the stern of the scow was a heavy steel ring, to match a similar pair of rings on the power boat even with the front thwart. The scow and power boat were coupled together at these rings with block and tackle, and a pair of blocks rigged at each side could be pulled tight to keep the scow straight ahead of the power boat. One of the poling boats was lashed to the side of the scow, the other two on each side of the power boat, so that the five boats made a tight cluster with the power boat inside.

As we left Fort Yukon on the first of July, Dad, Bill, and Pete rode the front of the scow, each with a poling stick, watching for snags, logs, or shallow water. Their poles were pike poles with the steel hook sawed off, leaving only the spike at the end; a hook would have caught on a lot of things under water and caused trouble. John ran the power boat. The dogs and the rest of us just rode.

On the Fourth of July, on a bar in Black River, we popped

firecrackers and threw rocks in the water, and wound up the day by eating a box of chocolates that Mom had saved for the occasion. Until then, the trip had been a picnic, for though the Porcupine was fairly swift, with many riffles, it was three hundred yards to three quarters of a mile wide in places, and our cluster of boats traveled easily, hugging the cutbank side for deep water on the bends and avoiding the gravel and sand-bars on the inside. The water was crystal-clear. Spruce were thick on the cutbank sides of the bends, willows and cotton-woods on the bars. Along the whole length of the Porcupine that we traveled, there were no hills.

As we turned up Black River the country and the water changed. Black River was a slower stream, the color of weak tea from the weeds along its edges and in the lakes that drained into it. All along one bank there were long grassy slopes, with cutbanks or gravel bars on the other. In some places grass came down to the water's edge on both sides, and where the grass grew out into the water, or in the mouths of grassy sloughs, we got good pike fishing. Along both rivers, getting more numerous as we went upriver, there were drift piles.

A week out and a hundred and sixty miles up Black River, we came to Pete Nelson's cabin and stopped to unload his outfit and uncouple his boat. Then we went on with John and Bill O'Brien and the four boats.

By the time we got to where Orange Creek and Salmon Fork came together to make Black River we were in a different kind of country. On the Salmon the cutbanks were covered with spruce as they were on the Porcupine, but there was a good deal of white birch on the higher ground, and the wide, clean gravel bars were backed with willows. Back of those were tall cottonwoods, and there were cottonwoods along the heads of the bars. At the lower ends of the bars, in the sloughs, beaver cut their winter food among the cottonwoods. Trails went up the banks to their wood yards, where stumps were standing about a foot high as if an axman had been at work.

Near the mouth of the Salmon green ridges and rolling hills lay back from the river, but as we went on up the ridges became higher, and rocky bluffs poked out. The hills were covered densely with spruce, birch, and aspen that made a solid green cover except where white trunks of birch and aspen showed through. Drift piles along the river were more frequent, and the current was stiffer.

One day we came to a shallow place where the water caught the front of the scow and turned us crosswise of the stream. The propeller of the power boat was on the rocks, the front of the scow rammed the bank. The two boats jackknifed, straining the hook on the pulley so that we had to land and put on the one extra pulley we had. John decided that we had better take the boats apart and line them over the riffle, he taking the power boat up through the narrow, crooked channel while Hazel, Dad, and I helped Bill O'Brien with the scow.

We worked the line along the low cutbank and around the brush until we had a straight pull on the scow, though we could not see it for the willows. Then we hauled while Bill O'Brien poled. He was a two-hundred-and-forty-pound man, but this was different from poling a boat loaded with three or four hundred pounds. This was a big scow with three or four tons aboard. He tried poling it from the back as he would have a poling boat, but the front of the scow would not stay out in the current; the line pulled it ashore. A man at the front would have helped but he didn't have one. Eventually he went up and tried to pole from the front by himself. He shoved the front off and the current shot the scow across the river onto the bar side, where we could see it. Then he tried to hold it close to the bar while we pulled it up, but as he came around the short turn of the river the current caught the other side and Bill couldn't hold against it. The scow shot across the river again and hit the cutbank.

Out of sight behind the willows, he yelled for slack, and we gave it to him. Then he yelled, "Hold it!" and we heard him rattling around in the boat. Then he yelled, "Let her go! We've got a hole in the scow. Turn the rope loose."

When we let go he poled over to the bar again, and John landed the power boat to help him. The scow had slammed against a buried log just below the waterline, and already had a foot of water in it. John and Bill stuffed up the hole with gunny sacks, clothes, and a light blanket, pumped the water out, and brought the scow back to where we had started at the foot of the riffle. The rest of the day we spent sorting things out and spreading them on the gravel bar to dry. About half our outfit was wet. The bar was covered with our winter food supply, and every willow was hung with clothing. What was worst, my baby brother's colored doll had melted inside a trunkful of clothing. We had to wash everything that was in the trunk, and the doll was nothing but a smear.

2. MOSQUITOES AND A BURN

EVENTUALLY the water rose, and we passed the riffle and went on until John said we were only twenty miles below his home cabin. There we met another riffle with water too low to pass, and while we sat there on the bar waiting for a raise we got initiated into what our new home would be like.

For one thing, mosquitoes. We couldn't go into the brush for firewood without being met by millions of them, but the only thing we could do about the mosquitoes on the bar was to build smudge fires, and for those we had to get wood. John said we had to build smudges for the dogs too or the mosquitoes would drive them crazy. They were tied to the willows, and by now they were all digging and rolling their heads in the damp sand.

After a while we had gathered enough wood to build six big bonfires in a circle around the dogs, and the woods were filled with smoke. Back at our own campfire Mom was preparing supper and Bill O'Brien was telling mosquito stories.

He told how he had been hunting muskrats in the Porcupine Flats one spring and had found a calf moose that the mosquitoes had killed. And he told about an even worse time on the upper Porcupine River, in Yukon Territory. He had come over the hill from the head of Salmon River and was using dogs for pack animals. No matter where he went he couldn't get away from the mosquitoes. They even followed him out into the middle of large lakes and sat on the gun sights so thick he couldn't see to shoot the rats. He dug deep holes in the ground for his five dogs, but in spite of all he could do, one dog was dead in the morning. Then two more died. To protect him during the night he took Tag, a borrowed dog, inside his mosquito net, but later he awakened to see Tag snarling over him, ready to jump, and he realized that the dog was crazy from the torment of the mosquitoes. He spoke gently to him, calmed him, and took him outside the tent and shot him. The only survivor among his five dogs was Momo, who lived only because the bugs couldn't get through her thick, long fur.

On that bar we kept fires going steadily for three or four days before we got a break in the clouds of mosquitoes. After that we had to build fires several more times when the pests got thick again, but sometimes we could sit around the camp-fire and listen to John tell about the country and not be bothered very much by the bugs.

John told us about a big burn, not more than two or three hundred yards back of camp, that ran for miles up and down the river, and Hazel and I set out one afternoon to see what a burn looked like. We crossed the narrow slough between the bar and the main bank on a two-log bridge we had built our-selves, and went through the willows and up the little bank into a mass of alder brush and fallen trees that were all a gray-blue color with black blotches on them. Poles were criss-crossed over niggerheads and entangled with very small spruce trees and the alder brush, and we could not see more than thirty or forty feet in any direction, but we went on, deter-mined to find the burn.

Soon we came to many little green-leaved bushes about a foot high, with very pretty berries of a chalky blue on them. They were so pretty that we forgot the burn and broke off some bushes to make bouquets.

Before long we heard Dad calling. He had tracked us to the edge of the flat and lost our tracks where we had walked along on the down poles. We answered and started home, and when we reached camp and gave Mother the bouquets we had picked she told us they were blueberries, and very good to eat. She asked us if we had found the burn, and we said no, only a lot of brush and wind-felled trees with no limbs on them, and niggerheads, and these bushes.

Dad and John started to laugh, and Dad said, "When I called them home, these kids were at least a quarter of a mile out in the burn picking berries like a couple of young bears."

We protested, "But Papa, there weren't any ashes out there!"

It took a while before we lived down walking right through a burn looking for it.

3. MOOSE HUNT

Two WEEKS we camped on the bar between the burn and the river, and fought mosquitoes and waited for higher water. My baby brother was sick, apparently with some infection in his kidneys, and he was still sick when we got rain and saw the water starting to rise and hurried to pack up for a try at the riffle. He didn't like the bar or the mosquitoes and was very happy to be on the scow again and on the way.

Two hours after we started he was dead. We buried him in a gravel bank that was covered with small green spruce trees, the ground white with caribou moss and spotted with green cranberry bushes loaded with red berries. These were low-bush cranberries, very short and flat on the ground. They cuddled down in the white moss as if it were warm and cozy there.

So the first thing we made at our new home was a grave. Then we went to our task of unloading the boats and putting everything in the cache. While the water was still high, John took Bill O'Brien twelve miles upriver to his cabin. As soon as he returned, he and Dad started building another room on John's one-room cabin.

While the new room was being built we lived in John's old cabin, but some of us had to sleep in the tent. The weather that fall was cold and rainy. Before the cabin was finished the water began to rise, and it kept on rising until in three days it was over the banks, and a foot deep in the house. We kids stayed marooned in the bunks while Mother, Dad, and John paddled around in hip boots doing the daily chores. For four days we had our meals served to us in the bunks. When the river went down, we found the scow high and dry on the bank, where Dad and John blocked it up and left it for the winter. The power boat and poling boat they left in the water.

Time was going fast, and there was much to be done to get ready for the winter. By the first of September the cabin was finished, and on that first day of the hunting season Dad killed a moose. We were all very busy picking cranberries and putting them down for the winter, but we needed more meat — at least two more big moose and some caribou if possible. Dad was too crippled to hunt much. That meant that John had to do it, and Hazel and I, twelve and eleven, went along to help John.

Our first moose hunt, just after the first of September, lasted ten days. We loaded the poling boat with tent, bedding, and grub, and took two axes, a hammer, and some nails so that we could build a cache if we got meat. John tied one end of the trackline to each end of the boat, and another rope on to the trackline so that it would slip. Then if he pulled on the bow rope the boat came in to shore, and if he pulled on the stern rope it went out. All of us walked along shore and pulled.

The first day we went six miles upriver and camped on a gravel bar. After the tent was set up and dinner over, we climbed the bluff and looked for moose. We saw three, but they were all cows and we did not want them. It was the first time that Hazel and I had ever been up on a high hill like that where we could look all over the country below, and we were surprised at how much we could see.

Just below us was a beaver slough with a beaver house in it. We watched the beaver cutting branches from a big cottonwood they had gnawed down, and then taking the branches over to the feed pile, diving with them, and tucking them under the branches already there. The water was so clear that we could see every move the beaver made, even when they were on the bottom of the slough under six or eight feet of water. The four big beaver and three kits worked all the time we watched, and they were still working when we started back to camp.

That night about eight, when we were sitting around the campfire talking about all the things we had seen, we heard a loud *plop*. Hazel and I jumped, and Hazel said, "Somebody is shooting around here."

"That was a beaver," John said. "He don't want us around. Take a good look and you'll see him out there in the river."

All we could see on the darkening river was a silvery V-shaped mark, and at the very front end a black ball. That was the beaver's head, John said. As we watched we saw a big spray of water go up, and there was the loud plop again. We jumped again. We couldn't help it. "What are you jumping about?" John said. "He can't shoot you."

The beaver was still slapping the water when we went to bed. It seemed strange to us to spend a night without Mom around.

The next day we camped on a little island at the mouth of a beaver slough where the water was deep and quiet, the surface constantly broken by jumping grayling. We would have given anything for a fly hook and line, but we hadn't brought tackle along. After a quick lunch of moose steaks, bread, and tea, John said, "I'm going up on the hill and look around. You want to go with me or stay in camp?"

We wanted to go. Hazel asked, "Can I take my gun?"

"Not this time," John said. "You'd get too tired carrying it."

From up on the hill we could look across the river valley. We saw a cow and a calf moose, then off to one side a big bull. After a while another big bull came over the ridge. Just before they met they stopped, lowered their heads, shook themselves, and pawed the ground. Then they ran at each other as hard as they could go. Their huge horns clashed together with a sound that echoed clear over to where we were. The impact threw both bulls off balance, but they recovered and ran back fifty feet or so to turn and come at each other again. After they had gone through that performance half a dozen times, we saw a third bull come out and start chasing the calf.

"Gee God," John said, "let's us go over and see if we can chase some of those moose around too."

It was about a mile over there. We went around the hillside until we got pretty close. John told us to stay back, and if he put his hand up, to stop and stand still until he called us.

When he raised his hand we stopped. John sneaked ahead,

and in a minute we heard five or six quick shots. Then he called us. A cow and a calf moose were standing on a little ridge, watching us. Between them and us lay a big bull.

By the time we had skinned him and cut up the meat it was dark. We ourselves had no idea where camp was or how to get there. We thought it was wonderful the way John found his way back in the darkness.

Next day we had the job of caching the meat and packing some of it out to the boat. On the birch hillside covered with ripe cranberries we found two spruce trees about eight inches in diameter, and near them a birch about the same size. John cut off all three trees about fifteen feet above the ground while Hazel and I cut poles for a platform. By six that evening we still didn't have it done. Each of us took a pack of meat and fat and we started back for the boat. There were lots of niggerheads. John could walk right along through them, but we had troubles. We were too short to step across the water between the niggerheads, and so each time we had to walk around them. Many times we fell down with our packs of meat, and had to help each other up. John wouldn't give us a chance to catch up to him. He would wait until we were almost up, and then he'd start out again. We were dead tired before we were halfway back to camp.

Once Hazel fell down and when she tried to get up, wedged herself in between two big niggerheads, flat on her back. She couldn't even turn over. I took hold of her hands and put my feet against hers and pulled, but when I had her almost up our hands slipped. She went back where she had been and I went flat on my back between two other niggerheads. Neither of us could get up, and to make it worse we were both lying in water. John was out ahead a little way.

We yelled until he came back. But when he saw us he laughed as though he would die.

He said, "Why don't you get up?"

We said we couldn't. "Help us," Hazel said. "We're getting all wet."

"That's a hell of a place to lie down," John said. Then he laughed some more.

Finally he helped us up and we made it into camp, but we could hardly move when we got in. Right away John said, "Who's going to cook supper? I want to rest awhile."

I looked at Hazel, and she looked half dead. "I will," I said.

Hazel went to sleep. When we woke her up and told her dinner was ready she started to cry. "I don't want to eat," she said.

"Let her go," John said. "She can't take it."

So she went without dinner that night. The next day was just like the one before it, and again she went to bed without any dinner. But that day we finished the cache, put the meat on it and covered it with the moosehide, and took a load of meat back to camp. When John shot a buck caribou the next day, a couple of miles upriver, he said he guessed we'd take the caribou and the moose meat we had packed out and go home. For two days we drifted down the river, until we saw Mom and Dad cutting winter wood on the bank.

While we were gone, Dad had killed a caribou on the bar just below the cabin. That gave us one moose and two caribou, but John thought we ought to have one or two more to be safe. After a week at home cutting wood and building a pair of bobsleds to haul it on when we got snow, the three of us started upriver again. Again we camped on the six-mile bar. Again we climbed the hill and sat on the bluff looking over the valley. This time we saw a bull moose coming downriver, about four miles away, and we hurried back to camp and John tapped the moose horn we carried in the boat to call moose with. For quite a while we waited, but when no moose came around, we ate dinner. In the middle of our talking and laughing John said, "Listen! What was that?"

We went outside the tent. There was a splashing in the dark, and by the faint light from the sky, reflected in the water, we saw the shadow of a bull moose trying to climb into the boat. John grabbed his rifle; the moose snorted and plunged to swim back across the river. He looked like a big root in the dark, for his horns were all we could see. John shot two or three times, and each time the fire flew ten or fifteen feet from the muzzle of the rifle, but the moose kept on going.

In the morning when we got to our little island we looked up the hillside for our cache, but couldn't see it, even with field glasses. John decided we had better go over and look. When we got there we found the cache only a pile of poles and a mass of mud. A bear had found it and had chewed off one of the legs and let the whole platform down on himself. There were brown hairs all over the poles. All around the foot of the three trees he had dug up the ground, caching meat and digging it up again. What he hadn't eaten he had buried.

John was mad. We looked around for the bear, but saw no sign of him, though we went over to the ridge beyond and sat down and watched the cache a long time. Finally

John took the field glasses and played them all around, and pretty soon he said, "There's the devil, right there by that little spring!"

He was only about three hundred yards away. John put down the glasses and picked up his rifle. After the first shot the bear thrashed around, after the third he lay still. He was a big yellow-backed bear, and he was dead when we came up to him. For years afterward his beautiful skin lay as a rug in front of Mother's bed.

That trip we got no caribou, and the bear didn't compensate for the moose meat we had lost. About the twenty-fifth of September we went on our third and last hunting trip of the season. The yellows and reds of fall were still bright among the spruces, but they were fading, and many of the trees were almost bare. The sky was a clear cold blue, the air cold except in the sun. Each night a little ice formed along the water's edge.

As soon as we were well away from home, Hazel said, "If we see a moose, can I shoot him?"

"Sure," John said.

Hazel and I were pulling the trackline while John poled and steered in the boat. We saw no game until about noon of the third day, when Hazel and I spotted a cow moose in the willows on a bar across the river. Just then a big bull walked down the bar, but screened behind the willows. We stopped, and I started coiling in the line while Hazel ran back to the boat for her rifle.

"Go on," John called. "That's a cow. We don't want her."

"There's a bull there too," I said.

The moose raised their heads and looked at us. The bull shook himself, but kept on coming toward the cow, feeding on the red willows. Finally John saw the bull and swung the boat ashore so Hazel could get her rifle. "Right behind the shoulder," he said.

Hazel started shooting. She must have emptied the magazine in her excitement, but when the gun was empty the moose was down. "I got him!" she yelled. "I got him, I got him!"

That night we camped in the willows by the moose, and next morning when we looked out of the tent the ground was white with two inches of snow. The camp robbers fluttering between the willows and the meat powdered down showers of snow from the willows. John said it was tracking weather, but we didn't want to get caught in the freeze-up, and since Hazel had got her moose we'd better hit for home while we could.

It was terribly cold sitting cramped in the boat with the camp stuff and with the moose head and the big horns on a box at the bow. We had to take turns rowing to keep from freezing solid. The shore was lined with slush ice floating in the water. Each little stick seemed to be sitting on a disk of ice that grew larger as the icy water lapped around it. In the open, the sun melted the snow off the trees and gravel bars, but in the shaded places ice kept forming steadily.

As we came near home Hazel said, "Gosh, we seem to be going awful slow."

We were all shivering and chattering, but every time she looked at the moose head sitting there in front of her she smiled.

At last we saw the smoke rolling up from the stovepipe, a really cheery sight. We landed so quietly that not even the dogs heard us until we were on top of the bank. As they jumped up to welcome us, John said, "Keep quiet, now!" and they never made a sound as we walked up through the tall grass to the cabin. The two birch trees beside the front of the house looked as though they had been undressed while we were away. Not a leaf remained on them.

Outside the door we stopped and sniffed the smell of boiling meat. Then we burst open the door and there were Mother, Dad, and Elsie, sorting onions to put the best in the cellar for the winter. They had sprouted all the potatoes, too, and a newly built toboggan hung high under the roof to dry the rawhide carryall. The warmth of the house on our cold faces and hands made us tingle and shiver.

"Mom!" Hazel said, "I killed a moose!"

4. FIRST WINTER ON THE SALMON FORK

THAT WAS the real beginning of winter for us, the first of the thirteen winters we were to spend in the cabin on the Salmon Fork. It was also the first experience we had with the real work and hardship of trapping. We still played like kids, but some of the time we had to work like grownups. From that winter I remember something about dolls and doll games, and quite a lot about moose.

We had a seven-by-seven tent for a playhouse in the yard of the cabin, and in it we put a small stove made of a gasoline tin, a spruce bough bed, a table made of poles, and some camp dishes Mom gave us. Sometimes we fried meat and boiled tea, and we had pieces of moosehide tied to trees near the tent to represent our dogs. Each piece of moosehide had a name. We hitched them to a gasoline box for a toboggan, and dragged them after us for a quarter of a mile or so down the trail while we set traps for squirrels, which we called marten. We told each other wild experiences we had with moose, bears, and wolves on our make-believe traplines.

Each of us had a boy's name, and used it entirely in these games. Hazel was Bob, Elsie was Jim, and I was Tom. We called the cabin the Roadhouse, and paid for the meals and lodging we took there with paper money we made out of cardboard. If one of us got mad at the others when we were not playing, she would go over to the play tent and light a fire and stay there till she got over it. Dad nicknamed the tent the "swearing closet."

One day when we were playing trappers I was Jim's wife. My two doll babies were in make-believe high chairs beside the stove. Mother called us to dinner and we all ran for the house, forgetting to shut the stove down. In a few minutes Dad looked out the window beside his bed, where he spent most of his time all crippled up by arthritis in the cold weather, and hollered, "Hey, you kids, your swearing closet's going up in smoke!"

We all rushed out and put out the fire, which had been started by a falling spark from the stovepipe. Nothing in the tent was hurt except the dolls. Their faces were covered with blisters from the heat of the stove, and from then on we told each other stories of the big fire that had left our children scarred for life.

We were too high up in the mountains for real muskrats around the cabin. There weren't any lakes near us. But every April we gathered up two-dozen small traps and started out with our moosehide dogs and gasoline-box toboggan to put out our muskrat lines. We set the traps under upturned roots and covered them with loose snow, just as we had set them for real rats on the Sheenjack. Each evening we went over our line and put small pieces of moosehide in the traps for rats, and each morning we hitched up our play dogs, two of us walking ahead of the moosehide lead dog to pull him along and one coming along behind the box toboggan like a driver, looking at the traps and taking out the make-believe muskrats.

Sometimes we hitched up real dogs and went for a real ride, and our playing got mixed up with the real. Somehow the real seemed to have a lot to do with moose. One day in mid-March we hitched up three dogs and started on the trail. They didn't want to go; we had to make a lot of noise yelling, and even take the whip to them a time or two. All at once they flattened out and started to run, and we grabbed the toboggan and yelled, "Hurry, boys, hurry!"

They plunged off the trail, and we saw the big, unreal head of a cow moose come up among them. I stepped on the brake as hard as I could, and yelled "Whoa!" Hazel and Elsie were riding in the toboggan. I stood on the brake and held the team, for I expected the moose to turn on us any second. She got to her feet, broke away from the dogs, and trotted away while Hazel frantically scrambled to get the rifle out from under herself and Elsie. The dogs spit out the wads of hair they had chewed off the moose, and started barking like mad. After a minute the moose made up her mind to run and not charge, and trotted off into the woods.

The other time I had a brush with a moose on the trail, things didn't go so quietly. I learned that winter to be scared of a moose, and I never got over it.

When the trapping season opened on November 1 John had put his own lines out and then had helped Mom with hers. The cold weather crippled Dad so that he could hardly get out of bed. Sometimes John ran the lines alone; sometimes Hazel or I went with him.

Fairly early in the season two Indians came to the house and asked if they could go to the end of our trapline on our trail, and put out their lines beyond ours. John told them to go ahead and use our trails and camps to get to where they wanted to trap. But after a couple of weeks they were back. One of them was sick and the other was taking him into town, and they wouldn't be able to get back to pick up their traps before the season closed. John agreed to pick up their traps for them, next time he ran our lines. That was one of the times I went along.

The Indians said their tent was eight miles beyond the end of our sideline. We got an early start, wanting to get there before dark, and to allow time for trouble in following their trail. But we had no trouble; our leader followed their trail all day, past three or four of the places where in the Indian fashion they had stopped to build up big fires and make tea. Indians will stop three or four times a day for tea; white men seldom do. Still we saw no tent. About dark we saw the heavy line of spruces that marked the river, and John said he bet the tent was in there. We came to the river, but still no tent. We did see a cow moose in the river, however, standing in snow five feet deep so that she was unable to run as we went by on the trail, which dropped down onto the channel, followed it for two or three hundred yards, and then went back up on the bank on the same side.

As we left the river we went through the big timber a little way, where the snow was shallower. I heard John say, "There's another moose, close to the trail," and then in a desperate voice, "and he's going to come!"

He yelled at the leader, "Hurry up, Rags!" The dogs jerked the toboggan ahead and I looked around to see not more than fifteen feet away the face and knees of a big bull moose. His eyes showed the whites all the way around, his ears were flat on his neck and he was coming straight for me in big jumps. I didn't have time to move from where I was sitting bundled up on the back of the toboggan before his cold wet nose hit me fair in the face. His knees hit the toboggan and turned it over. One foot went through the rawhide carryall and grazed my hip as I spilled into the snow. John was yelling at the moose, and the dogs were all barking. I lay still, scared to move and expecting the moose back any minute. When he didn't come I climbed out and headed for the nearest tree. I wanted something between him and me if he came again. But apparently he had gone on toward the river after upsetting us. John got the .44 pistol out of the toboggan, untangled the dogs, and we started on.

In a mile we came to the tent. I was still shaky, and every least noise made me jump. The tent didn't look like much protection, either, from anything. It was the worst I ever tried to live in. Sparks had fallen on it and burned small holes until the roof was a sieve. There was a spot of snow inside for every hole in the roof, and when we blew out the candle and went to bed the holes looked like that many huge stars. It was like sleeping outside.

As luck would have it, it snowed again that night and in the morning our beds were spotted with snow. We took up the Indians' traps and started back, but when we passed the place where the moose had charged us I was shivering cold and sweating at the same time, afraid he would be there again. When we were past the place I kept looking behind every tree. I wanted to run. It seemed that the dogs, trotting right along, were hardly moving.

We had a poor catch that winter of 1928–29. Toward the end of April we began helping with the skinning of wolves, kept frozen until then, and with cutting meat into strips for drying. We had to fix the boats for the trip to town, and put away the toboggans and trapping equipment for the summer. As soon as the ice was out of the river we started trapping beaver until we had our limit, which was ten each, and then we loaded dogs, furs, and camping equipment into the boats for the trip to Fort Yukon.

The next time we came up the Porcupine and Black and Salmon, Dad was not with us. He was in the hospital in Fort Yukon, and he never came out except when they moved him to the Pioneers' Home in Sitka the next year. I never saw him again. When we went up the river in the summer of 1929 after only three weeks in Fort Yukon, we were old John, past sixty, Mother, and us three girls, thirteen, twelve, and ten. The menfolks were all gone — all three boys and now Dad. That left the womenfolks to do the work for the family. For the next twelve years our lives were an unvarying routine: up the river in the summer; a fall of woodcutting, meat-getting, toboggan-building, berrypicking; a long, hard, cold winter of running the traplines; a spring of beaver trapping, wolf skinning, closing-up; a fast trip downriver; a brief few weeks in Fort Yukon, and up the river again.

Since I was a summer child, my birthday nearly always happened while we were headed up the Porcupine or Black toward the home cabin. My present on my twelfth birthday was a .30–.40 Krag rifle.

III. Upriver

1. TWENTY-FIVE DOGS ON THE RIVER

In a way, the upriver trip every summer was our vacation.
Pete Nelson always came with us, and except for one year
when he got mad at us about something and went up alone
in his poling boat, Bill O'Brien came too. Both were old
men — Bill seventy or so, and Pete about John's age. Pete
was slender, very careful about fires, very neat in everything
he did. Bill was a very large man, with white hair and pink
cheeks. Both were good company, in different ways. We
could never really feel in a hurry because, in spite of Pete's
hustling desire to get back to his own house, we could always
count on being stalled by low water enough times so that the
trip out would take us anywhere from a month to two
months. Ten days of steady running time would have done
it, which meant that during the other twenty to fifty days
we were either in trouble, and having plenty of excitement
to keep us awake, or loafing on some gravel bar with nothing
much to do.

Our outfit was pretty much the same from year to year,
but as the seasons went by we improved the system a little.

In the summer of 1933 we took the Universal engine out of storage and the following spring we rigged it in the scow, so that after that season the power boat and the scow could run independently if they had to. We put a block of wood eight inches square on the stern of the scow for the power boat to rest against when they were coupled. This also kept the scow's propeller from hitting the nose of the power boat when it was raised to go across shallow water. The new arrangement was a good rig when the scow's propeller was on the rocks, for by the time the power boat's propeller hit in the shallow water, the scow would usually be over.

Of course there were places where both boats were in shallow water, and then we had to fall back on the poles. I handled the scow engine while John and Elsie handled the Kermath and steered the boats. Mother, Hazel, Bill O'Brien, and Pete Nelson were in the front of the scow to help with their poles when needed. Their main job was to keep watch for snags, floating driftwood, and shallow water.

Putting in the second engine made many of our difficulties lighter, but it gave us some new ones too, and the difficulties got multiplied as our dogs increased from year to year. We had started out with seven; by 1933 we had eighteen, and they took up a lot of room in the boats. Also, now we needed thirty-six cases of gasoline to make the trip, instead of twenty. We never went out of Fort Yukon without a load on.

The scow always held the grub supply for the winter, canned goods packed around the engine, flour and cornmeal on the floor in front of it — twelve hundred pounds of the one and five hundred of the other. Our thousand pounds of sugar went with the paper cartons and things easily damaged on top of the eight cases of gasoline, right behind the engine, with the dogs' fish on top of it all.

The power boat carried twenty-eight cases of gasoline with twelve dogs riding on top of them and the cans we needed for feeding and watering the dogs scattered in every available space. As long as Pete and Bill were with us, each of them carried some of our dogs in his poling boat. Pete had no dogs of his own — he had been bitten when he was a child, and he was scared of them — but Bill had seven. That made twenty-five dogs to be loaded and unloaded and fed and kept from fighting. The last was the hardest: the dogs never tried to bite us, but whenever dogs from different teams got put together they could be in a fight in a half second. A good thick green willow club about three feet long generally quieted them in a hurry, though.

It is astonishing how much nuisance twenty-five dogs can be when the weather is bad or the river rises suddenly or the camping place isn't everything it should be. A good camping place is a large gravel bar where the water is deep enough to get the boats in close, with willows large enough to tie all the dogs to. But such a place is hard to find, and plenty of times we had to camp on something a little less than perfect.

There was an evening when we made camp on a narrow gravel bar under an undercut bank about six feet high. The beach was without any room to tie the dogs, and we had to take them out on top, into the tangle of rosebushes, willows, fallen trees, and berry bushes. In order to save climbing the bank too many times, each girl took out four dogs at once, but when we tried to lead them up the bank we found that the dogs jumping around us made it impossible to climb at all. I finally turned my four loose and scrambled up the bank and started calling, "Jump, Happy!"

Happy made a wild leap at the bank, and I reached down and caught him by the scruff of the neck and pulled him up.

Then I heard Elsie call, "Jump, Prince!" and saw that she was doing the same thing I had done. And then I looked along the bank and there was Hazel, without any of her dogs, climbing the bank. That meant that ten dogs, from three different teams, were loose on the beach and in ten seconds there could be a first-class dogfight.

"Lie down!" I said to my own dogs, as quietly as I could. I called to Katy, my leader, and told her to jump, but she was so small that she had to try three times before I could catch her and pull her up. Jerry and Pinto made it in two leaps each, and I tied them all to trees near the edge of the bank, partly because the farther back in you went the thicker the mosquitoes were, and partly so I wouldn't have to carry their suppers too far through the tangle.

As soon as the first twelve dogs were tied up we went back and got the others. Hazel went to set up camp, while Elsie climbed the bank again and I passed her up the empty water cans, and then cans of water to fill them. While she watered them, I brought dried salmon and tossed it up on the bank and finally I climbed up and helped her feed the twenty-five of them. We were not very fond of dogs by the time we got down out of there with our shoes full of dirt and scratches all over our hands and arms.

Sometimes in bad places we could use the dogs on the trackline, but most of the time they were plain nuisances. If we had to load them into the poling boat and take them across a shallow, they generally had to jump into the water at the very shallowest part, and then jump into the boat again after we had passed it. Then they shook all over us.

There were so many of them they were hard to handle if they had to be led past any place. Once as we were going through an old shallow channel we had to unload them, and John took four and I took six to lead them along the bank. I tied the chains around my waist to keep the jumping dogs from pulling away. They were big dogs, and strong pullers; the six of them outweighed me by about three to one, and I had my hands full.

John saw what I had done and said, "Untie those, for Lord's sake. If they start fighting you'll be torn up."

I laughed and showed him the stick I was carrying. "You'd be surprised what a difference just a little stick makes."

Just then Pinto jumped ahead of me and I hit him. As he jumped back he hit Jack, knocking him against Dick. Dick snapped, and the fight was on. I had been too lazy to muzzle the dogs with string. A third dog joined the fight, with the other three pulling the other way. My stick broke on the third hit. The dogs swirled and snapped and rolled, entirely too close for comfort, and I could not loosen the chains that tied them to me. The only thing I could do was to keep kicking at them and try to work myself over to a stout stick that lay ten feet away. Excited dogs were pulling in every direction, and it was hard to keep my feet. The fight stirred up all the other dogs so that the rest of the family had all they could do to handle their own, and could not help me. I staggered along, kicking the fighters out of the way and dragging the others, until I could almost stoop and reach the stick. Then they pulled me over. My falling jerked them almost on top of me and I expected to get bitten any second, but I managed to crawl the last yard and get my hand on the stick.

As soon as they felt that club on them they quieted, and I muzzled them with string as I should have done in the first place. I didn't find out until then that Hazel, landing her boat in order to help me, had had her pole knocked out of her hand by an excited dog and had run two hundred yards back downstream before she could recover it.

Let any emergency arise, let the weather get bad or the river rise fast, and the dogs could be depended on to complicate everything. We were camped once on a bar two or three miles below the mouth of the Salmon. It had been raining for three days, and the water was rising. The sky was full of dark gray clouds, with right overhead a few spots of bright blue that closed and opened again. By noon the water had risen enough for us to go on, but after we had gone a mile it began to rain again. We pulled ashore at the first bar, set up the tarp over the scow, tied the dogs to roots well back on the bar, and crawled into the scow and lay down with robes over us. We didn't have a stove on the boat, and in the cold, driving rain a campfire was impossible.

About midnight the dogs whined and fussed. It was still raining, and so dark that Hazel and I could hardly see to get around when we got up to find out what was the matter. We crawled out to take a look at the dogs and all we could see was the dark shine of water. Four dogs were on top of the roots they were tied to, and three or four more were standing up to their bellies in the ice-cold muddy river. The rest were on higher ground.

We put on our overalls and hip boots and waded out. The high ground could hold no more dogs than it already had. We had to put the wet ones in the power boat, and they were so happy to see us that they jumped up on us and wagged their tails and threw water and mud all over us. While we swore and slapped at them they put up big wet paws to shake hands, and shook themselves until we were as wet as they were, and shivering just as bad.

Then the rest of the dogs got the idea we were going on, and howled and barked, and two of them broke loose and came splashing through the water to add to our shower bath. We put them in the power boat too, and went back to bed.

2. FISHING

TWENTY-FIVE DOGS take a lot of feed, much more than we could generally carry. At every stop we had to rustle food for them, and food generally meant fish. Pete Nelson, though he didn't like dogs, was crazy about fishing. A lot of our fun in the summer months was fishing with Pete.

He could get so excited if he hooked a pike that sometimes he tore the hook clear out of the fish's mouth, until I told him he'd do better to drag the fish out than to try to yank him. "Walk back from the river and pull him out," I said. After that whenever he hooked a big pike he would turn around, put the pole over his shoulder, and run back toward the woods until the fish was on the beach. Then he'd grab a club and run back, kneel over the fish, holding it between his knees and saying, "Now, now, you hold still!" Then he'd raise the club and whack the fish on the head. "Oh, I'll bump you!" he'd say. "I'll bump you and I'll bust you." He really liked to fish. The only things he saw wrong with it were the mosquitoes and the jackfishes' teeth, on which he tore his fingers as often as not getting the hook out.

Generally when we went fishing we took Pete's poling boat and went upriver and fished down, one of us fishing from the drifting boat and the others working down along the banks, fishing all the grassy stretches and the mouths of all the little sloughs and creeks. Some days we caught sixty or seventy pike with hook and line, and a third that many more with the net. If we did that well, we wouldn't have to fish again for a couple of days.

We didn't always do that well, but Hazel and I could always catch more than Pete or John, and as for Bill, he hardly ever caught much.

Black River just above the mouth of the Salmon was good pike water because the river had grassy banks and the water was slow, with lots of weeds along the edges. After Hazel and I took thirty or forty pike a day out of those weeds, one day Bill took the poling boat and allowed that he'd go up Black River and get a load of them pike too.

He was gone all day, and came back with one little one. "I guess you got all the pike that's up there," he said. "I went up Black River four miles and floated down the middle and fished all the way. Next time I'll go get me a bear."

We had to show Bill on that one. Next morning Mother and the three of us girls took the boat and started for the same place. Bill said there wasn't any use. He was sure that stretch of Black River was fished out. But we went anyway, and after we had poled four miles upstream Elsie and I each took one bank of the river and Mother fished from the boat while Hazel handled it. After Elsie and I had fished the best places, the boat crossed back and forth and fished them over again and picked up the fish that Elsie and I had left on the bank. The mosquitoes were around us in clouds all day, and the temperature was eighty above, and no breeze, but we wouldn't quit for that. By the time we drifted to the mouth of the Salmon we had forty-one pike, enough to feed the dogs for two days.

Bill came down to meet us, laughing fit to die, like a twinkly Santa Claus with his pink cheeks and his white hair and beard. He shut one eye and laughed some more. "Well, how about all those fish?" he said.

The bottom of the boat was covered with them, but as we had planned to do, we didn't say anything. I jumped out with the rope to tie the boat. "Here," Bill said, "I'll tie it for you." He was just full of good will, thinking he had a big joke on us.

"I can tie the darn boat," I said. "You get the fishpoles out of it."

He walked over, still laughing, but when he looked in and saw Mother and the two girls up to their knees in pike he sobered right down. "Where in hell did you get all them fish?"

"Black River," we said. "You know the place."

So Bill decided he wouldn't fish that stretch any more. We had got all the fish there were in it. "No use me going up there no more," he said. "I'll go get me a black bear tomorrow."

One of the hardest summers for getting fish was the one when Bill was mad at us and had gone up alone, and we had left our own poling boat at the winter camp. That meant that after we left Pete Nelson at his cabin we had to fish from the power boat, which was a heavy, chunky thing to drag up the river by hand. The ironwork on the stern hung up on the riffles and it took us hours to make three or four miles.

To cap the trouble we were having with the boat, the fishing was unusually bad. In a whole day we might get only four or five small pike, and that year we had fifteen dogs to feed. On one such day, at five-thirty in the evening, we had only four pike. "Be careful," John kept telling us. "Sneak up on them. Don't scare the fish away."

Hazel was fishing with a large bait hook and I had a small spinner. She always went ahead of me, because we were afraid that if there was a big fish around he might take my spinner and break loose. I was cleaning up the little ones, or intending to.

She cast out by a big root and got a strike. "Hey, that's a big one!" she said, and cast again. This time a fish took it, and she hauled him in toward shore, a pike about two feet long.

Right behind him as he came into the shallow water I saw a big wake. I couldn't believe my eyes, because there with his mouth open was a huge pike, ready to grab that two-foot pike on Hazel's hook. As she lifted her fish out, the big one splashed and turned back toward the root.

"Cast again!" I said to Hazel. "There's another one out there four times as big as this one."

"Oh, shut up," she said. "They don't grow that big."

"Fish for him!" I said. "He's out there."

She tried three or four times, but didn't get a strike. "Your whale doesn't seem to be around."

"He *is!*" I said. I still couldn't get over the way he had looked in the water, like a log. "You watch while I toll him in, and when he comes, I'll yank my spinner out and you catch him with your big hook. Watch now."

I cast away out by the root and pulled toward the shore. All at once the water walled up behind my spinner. I jerked, but too late. He had it. In spite of all I could do he started dragging me toward the water. "Hazel, help!" I yelled.

She grabbed my pole and we both pulled, but still we slipped toward the water. Then the fish turned and came toward shore. We snatched in the slack, and once in the shallow water he lost his great power, so that we pulled him out, fighting and flopping, onto the bank. All Hazel could say was, "Gosh, oh gosh, what a jackfish!" and John was yelling, "Don't let him get away!"

I didn't say anything. I was too surprised that my little spinner had held him. He was even bigger on shore than he had looked in the water. He was over four feet long, and his head was eight inches broad. We had no way of weighing him, but he fed eleven hungry dogs.

If we weren't fishing for pike, we were casting with a fly rod for grayling, and if we weren't after grayling we were trying for salmon. After we got busy and wove a salmon net during a long wait on a bar one year, we caught a good many, though we didn't allow for shrinkage in the net, and the holes shrank up too small to let the bigger king salmon in. Most of what we caught were small king salmon and the dog salmon that ran until later in the fall. We could always depend on catching a lot of mosquitoes, and sometimes depend on getting good and cold.

The water in the Salmon River especially was always icy-cold. Because we often fished late if we needed dog feed badly, we were likely to be wet and shivering as the sun went down, and still a long way from home. I remember one such evening when Hazel and I were out with John. The mosquitoes were as bad as I ever saw them, but they got worse as soon as we went into the timber to rustle wood for a fire to warm up by and smoke the bugs before starting home. A million more gnats and mosquitoes came right out of the woods with us. We stood over the fire and almost blistered our faces, but our backs stayed cold, our wet clothes touched a new spot every time we moved, and the mosquitoes got thicker and thicker in spite of the smoke.

Besides wearing hats, we had our heads covered with bandannas, but the mosquitoes still got into our noses, eyes, and mouths. We wore canvas gloves to protect our hands, but the mosquitoes gathered in a black mass on our backs and stung through our shirts, and the gnats got in under the bandannas and around our ears and into our eyes. Our eyes were all swelled, and blood ran down our faces. We even jumped through the leaping flames in the hope that the pests would follow us and get burned up. A lot of them did, but that didn't make any difference in the number around us. In twenty minutes they had put us on the run for home, but things weren't much better there. They were biting like mad, the way they do before a rain, and every bite was like a bee sting. When things get like that there is nothing to do but cover up and sit it out until rain, or wind, or something else chases the mosquitoes back into the woods.

If we had good luck fishing, and got dog feed for a few days ahead, Hazel, Elsie and I could go exploring. On such trips we always took one big rifle, in case we met a bear, plus a .22, a belt ax, and our pocket knives. We were interested in anything, but especially in materials we could make things of. Often we came back with our arms loaded full of cottonwood bark, which we carved into little dishes or animals. Any time we saw good clean birch trees we brought a load of birch bark home. And we kept our eyes open for berry patches, for these were the sources of our winter fruit supply, and fruit in winter when you have been living mainly on moose and rabbit can taste plenty good.

If we found any berries — red currants, cranberries, or anything else — we went out with Mom the next day and picked all we could get. After all our other work was done in the evening, Mom would set up two gasoline boxes close together for a table. On one she put a dishpan full of hot water with the quart Mason jars waiting in it, and on the other the berries. She washed the berries and cooked them down over the campfire, filled and sealed each jar, and left the jars to cool overnight. On our way upriver in the summers we accumulated a good many quarts of fruit this way, though some berrying came after we reached home. Every year we picked ninety or a hundred gallons of cranberries alone, to say nothing of blueberries, raspberries, and red and black currants.

Fishing and picking berries kept us busy most of the time even if we were hung up on a bar waiting for the raise, but Elsie and I found time to teach ourselves to swim in the ice-cold water of the river. The mosquitoes taught us to get under fast and stay under, even though the water took our breath. It was altogether too cold for the others.

Evenings around the campfire were the most peaceful time of day. Bill and Pete whittled aimlessly, or talked with Mom and John about experiences they had had, or they'd all plan how to get past a bad stretch of river. We girls might go off into the woods and come back with cottonwood or birch bark to carve into toys. We made full sets of miniature dishes, strings of cottonwood beads, many different kinds of little boats.

At mealtimes Bill and Pete each cooked for himself, but they often ate together for company, putting their grub boxes close together to sit on while they ate. For bread they ate crackers, as we did, but often too we baked bannocks, or "pan bread." The smallest ones that we made were about seven inches across and two inches thick. When we were waiting for the water to rise we might bake them in the morning and have them steaming-hot for breakfast, with fried potatoes and eggs and homemade marmalade or wild-berry jam on them. We never used coffee; tea took its place.

I well remember cooking breakfast over a campfire on a gravel bar on blazing-hot summer mornings with nothing to protect me from the sun, which was high in the sky by seven o'clock. In July it rose about three. There was always a smell of green cottonwood smoke, for we used a green cottonwood chunk for a side log, to hold the fire together and rest frying pans on. A bannock fire was built to reflect the heat outward, and thus into the cook's face. A small green cottonwood log was laid on top of two short stones and the fire built against the big cottonwood log, making an ovenlike place for the bannocks to cook in while the rest of the fire was used for other cooking.

When the meal was done, it was spread out on a small piece of canvas, and everyone sat around on the gravel with a plate in his lap and a cup beside him on the rocks. If anyone wanted water he dipped it out of the river.

On days when we were moving camp we generally ate a cold lunch on the boat, because if we went into the brush after wood we brought ten million mosquitoes back with us who gave us no peace while we ate. As long as we were on the river, or when we stopped on a large gravel bar, we were free of mosquitoes, but the minute anyone ventured near to the grass or brush he stirred up a lot of uninvited luncheon guests who were sure to do a lot more eating than he did. So we found it pleasanter to sit on the boat and eat cold bannocks, home-canned pickled caribou tongue, and fresh blueberries or red currant jam.

One summer John made a campstove out of two gasoline cans riveted together, with a door at one end and a stovepipe at the other, and I remember being left to take care of the dogs and the camp while the others went fishing. That day I took the last of the dry bread brought from town and made a bread pudding which I cooked by setting the pan up on four small rocks on top of the stove to keep the bottom from burning. I made bannocks, I boiled and mashed potatoes, and I boiled salted moose meat and laid it all out on the canvas on the ground as soon as the fishermen returned. There was very little left from that meal.

It was a hundred and sixty miles from Fort Yukon to Pete Nelson's cabin, which was about fifteen miles by airline, but two or three times that much by river, below the mouth of the Salmon. We could never reach it soon enough to suit Pete. He was always in a hurry. On the river he used to get up at four o'clock. If he had a tent, he packed it, and he rolled up his bedding. Most of the time he ate on his boat to save time, and when he was through he washed his dishes in the river and put them wet into the grub box. Then he would walk around the beach saying, "Gosh, you people are slow. Get a gait on. Let's get going."

The closer we got to his place the more excited he got, but he was always very happy. One time we were stuck downriver from his house, waiting for higher water, and I didn't get up until eight o'clock to start breakfast. Pete had been up since four, as usual. As I was baking the bannocks he came over and said, "Hey, what's the matter with those people? Aren't they ever going to get up?"

Before I could answer he added, "Oh, well, there's no use waking them up for the little piece of the day that's left now. They might as well stay in bed and get a good start on tomorrow." Then he laughed so hard it took him two minutes to stand up straight again.

About two bends before we reached his place he would begin to get nervous, and jump out on the deck of the scow with a poling stick in one hand and a coil of rope in the other and walk back and forth. I was running the scow motor once, and I saw him shift the coil of rope to the hand that held the pole, and start making wild gestures with the other hand. I could see that he was yelling, too, but the roar of the engines as we chugged steadily upriver drowned out his voice. We churned around the deep side of the bend under the cutbank, and his house came in sight on the high side, the little cabin at the edge of the woods. He pointed at it and shouted in a voice so loud it carried above the engine roar, "There's my house! Thank God for my house!"

He made signs to show us where to land, as though we had never been there before.

We unloaded his freight on the beach, at the foot of the trail which he had cut at an angle up the thirty-foot bank to his house and caches. Then we uncoupled his boat from ours and drifted back a hundred feet or so to make camp for the night.

It looked as if it might rain. Even before we took the dogs

out of the boats we put the tarp over the scow, while Pete at his place started packing stuff up the trail and stowing it away under cover. Elsie and I asked Mom, as soon as we had the dogs tied, if we could go help Pete so his things wouldn't get wet. She told us to go ahead.

When we went over, Pete looked up and said, "What do you want? Have you got the dogs all fixed up? You got to take care of those dogs. Remember, they can't talk."

"No," Elsie said, "but they can make plenty of noise."

"Forget the mutts," I said. "Could you use some help?"

"You bet I could," he said. "Here, take these beans. Thank God for the beans."

Every time he handed us something to lug up the bank he thanked God for it. "Here, take a sack of flour. Thank God for the flour. Case of corn. Thank God for the corn. Sugar. Thank God for the sugar." We had most of the stuff up when a blue-black cloud came over. Pete looked up and said, "Get a gait on. It's going to rain and get my stuff all wet."

We rushed down the bank and met Hazel coming up with a hundred-pound sack of flour on her shoulder. Pete stopped and clapped his hand on his forehead and said, "Thank God for Hazel!"

He broke into a run down the trail. I grabbed another sack of flour, and Pete yelled, "You can't pack that. Take it out of the gunny sack and we'll pack it fifty pounds at a time."

"I can pack it," I said. "Get something else."

Hazel was already coming down the bank again. "Only two more loads," Pete yelled.

By the time I had dumped the sack of flour in the house, which was nearer than the cache, it was pouring down rain. I ran for the last load, threw my denim jacket over a cardboard carton to keep it dry, and staggered it up the bank. Hazel got the last load of all. We could see Elsie and Pete looking out at us in the rain from the window of the house. "Hey!" Pete yelled. "Get a gait on. It's raining!"

We were all laughing as we set down our loads. "What's this?" Pete said.

"I don't know," I said. "I kept it dry, anyway."

He looked and laughed some more, pointing his finger at us. After about a minute he got out, "You like to drowned yourself to keep a few cans dry!"

"Soon as this quits we've got to get back and help Mom feed and water the dogs," Hazel said. That started Pete again. "Water the dogs," he said. "My God. Haven't they got enough water?"

We stood and laughed and watched the rain come down. When it let up a little and we started to go, Pete dug in his pocket and pulled out all the money he had. He gave Elsie and me a dollar each, and Hazel a half dollar. "Now I'm all right," he said. "Now I'm home and no money, but what's the good of money? No place to spend it till I get back to Fort Yukon next year."

He came down and sat around the campfire with us that night and told us how glad he was he didn't have another hundred and twenty miles to go to get home. And the next morning he came down and shook hands all around. "The only thing you got over me," he said, "you can go fishing some more. I'll never forget the times I've gone fishing with you girls. I have more fun on those trips than I have all the rest of the year. By gosh, I almost wish I was going on with you so we could go fishing some more!"

3. AN ARCTIC FIREBUG

No TRIP UPRIVER would have been complete without one of Bill O'Brien's fires. He was a very different kind of man from Pete — big, slow in his movements, drawling. He seemed to fear nothing, and he took his time about everything he did. Whenever we passed a big driftwood pile we would have to start worrying about Bill, because he seemed to have a mania for setting such piles afire. He said he did it to burn mosquitoes up.

One day while we were camped just a couple of miles above Pete Nelson's place Bill said he was going to set fire to the big drift pile that started at the water's edge a quarter of a mile below camp and was piled in against the trunks of the big spruce timber for a hundred yards or so back inland. We told him not to burn it under any circumstances, because for sure it would get out of control, and might burn miles of country right in the middle of Pete's trapline.

Bill said in his slow way, "Well, I guess you're right. I wouldn't want to burn Pete out."

"Besides," we said, "we can't move, and we've got five hundred gallons of gasoline aboard."

But a few days later we saw a big column of smoke rolling up down by the drift. Hazel yelled, "Hey, the drift pile is afire!"

"Aw, that's all right," Bill drawled. "Just burn up some bugs."

Mother and John came running out of the tent, and Mom said, "That's got to be put out right away."

By the time we could get down there, it was burning halfway to the tops of the tall spruces. The green boughs burned like oil; the sky was full of black smoke. John and I stayed with the boats, so we could take care of the dogs, and the others took axes and five-gallon cans to fight the fire with. Hazel and Bill went behind, and felled the big spruces that were not burning, as well as some that the fire had jumped. That made a kind of fire break. Then they all packed cans of water, and called to me to bring two more. We worked four hours before we had it under control. If it had gone twenty minutes longer we never would have stopped it. "By golly," Bill said, "I didn't think it would do that. I guess I shouldn't have started it."

But it didn't cure him. Next year he started two fires, one of which burned over twenty miles of country between the Salmon and Black Rivers. The second one almost trapped Mom and us girls in a blueberry patch.

Blueberries generally grow in niggerhead flats, and ninety per cent of a niggerhead flat is dry grass. One day when we were across the river from camp, picking berries about a mile out in the flat, Hazel yelled, "Hey, look! That darn Bill has set another fire."

"Oh," Mom said, "I wonder what now!"

After watching the smoke pour up for a while, we started picking again. The wind was blowing the smell of smoke toward us but we thought we would pick our pails full before going home. But pretty soon our whole flat was filled with smoke. Looking upriver I could see flames leaping about a mile above us. "Look at that!" I yelled. "He's set *this* flat on fire!"

"We've got to get out of here right now or we won't get out," Mom said.

We headed for the river as fast as we could, but the fire

was coming so fast that it would have beaten us there if the wind hadn't veered around and a thunder shower hadn't come up just at the right time. It poured down rain for an hour, and the wind blew from the north, so that the fire stopped and fizzled out, but it had already burned over two miles.

We asked Bill why he had started it, and he said, "There's lots of bugs in them niggerheads, and I didn't think it would go so far."

On Salmon River there was a big open flat in which a fire years ago had killed all the trees. They lay crisscrossed for miles, as dry as could be, with grass and fireweed growing thick around and through them. This place was one we liked, with the green grass rising out of the thick bed of light brown dry grass, and the bright red blossoms of the fireweed hiding all the down spruces. A little further on there were several very small lakes surrounded by bright green grass. We loved to watch the wind move through the grass and across the surface of the water.

Bill wanted to burn this beautiful place. One day when we were there with him he was all set to but he didn't have a match along, and he begged us to lend him one. We wouldn't. A week later, however, we saw the telltale column of smoke going up, and Mom said, "It looks like our firebug is at work again. I wonder where he's touched off the spark this time."

Hazel looked at me with anger in her eyes. "Damn him, I'll bet it's our pretty flat, the one with the lakes in it. The smoke is coming from the country between Salmon and Black River."

"You'd think he'd have more sense than that," Mom said. "Why, it would go for miles!"

In the late afternoon Bill drifted leisurely down to camp.

We asked him if he had had any luck fishing and he laid down the oars and said, "Not much luck. I got a dozen grayling and shot the hind leg off a b'ar."

"Where's the bear?" John asked.

"Oh, he ran off on three legs. Couldn't seem to hit him again."

Elsie said, looking very serious, "Did you say you shot the leg off a bear?"

"That's what I did. Big one, too."

"Why didn't you bring the leg home for dog feed?"

Bill looked at her as though she was crazy. "Well," he drawled, "I didn't shoot it clear off, and he ran away with it."

As he stepped from the boat, I saw a spark hole in his jacket. I put my finger on it. "How'd you get that? It looks as though you got too close to a fire sometime."

"Well, I'll tell you," he said, looking upriver toward the smoke. "Remember that grass flat I wanted to burn a little bit ago? I set it afire today. And you know, that grass burns fast. I went pretty well out into it before I set it afire, and when it started burning it went so fast I thought it would catch me before I could get to my boat. It went over those poles faster than I could. It just about got me. But I betcha it'll get a lot of bugs before it stops burning."

Hazel turned away, muttering, "The one it should have burned up got out too fast."

That was the way our summer trips went when we were held up, and there was always more time spent held up than on the river. But the traveling itself was often exciting, and if it wasn't exciting it was pleasant.

When we were under way, in easy water, everything got

quiet except for the steady roar of the engines, which seemed to be playing an endless, monotonous tune. It was hard to stay awake. I used to make up little poems to match their drone, for it seemed at times as though they were faintly singing, the sort of music where you can almost understand the words but not quite. My little poems would be tucked away in my catchall box for a few days and then tossed overboard to drift down the river. Today I have only one of them, and it isn't much of a poem.

The sun on the water tired our eyes, and its warmth on our bodies made us sleepier. Just about the time the hum of the engines would start turning into real words, I'd hear a sharp *crack!* and jerk awake to see Hazel putting her poling stick back in place. Each of us kept watch on the others, and if anyone started dozing we cracked the gunwale with a poling stick to bring him awake — not always in a good mood. Sometimes I got so mad at Hazel I could have knocked her overboard if she had been within reach. Boy! was I glad when I could get even by cracking the poling stick on the gunwale myself to wake *her* up or bring her back from far-away thoughts.

Sometimes we didn't need to be kept awake. It was no trouble at all to stay awake when the rain had driven us ashore on some narrow, half-flooded bar and we had to eat a cold supper and crawl in our wet clothes, without a fire, under our robes or under the tarp on the scow. On some of those nights I don't think I stopped shivering much before morning. And if the water rose suddenly, we were likely to have dog trouble, and be wading around half the night in hip boots. Or we got our stuff wet and had to lay over a day to spread everything out on a gravel bar to dry.

Once in a while we were luckier. I remember standing under the tacked-up pieces of canvas on the scow in a dripping rain, our clothes soaking wet, huddling around the fire in the gasoline-tin stove. Steam rose from us as if we were on fire. Mom said, "Why don't you girls change your clothes and get comfortable?"

"It's the changing part that gets me," Hazel said. "These clothes are just getting comfortable, as long as I don't move. It's too cold in that scow to change."

Mom insisted. The changing was every bit as bad as we expected, but once we were in dry clothes our teeth gradually stopped chattering and we were a lot warmer.

For two more days the rain poured down. Because the bar we were on was low and flat we had to pull out as soon as the water would let us get over the riffle, for otherwise our camp would have been flooded out. Still in the rain, we moved upriver to where an old cabin stood, and Hazel tied the boat rope to a spruce and ran up to look. She came back all smiles. "Mom, it's dry as a bone, not a single leak."

With a gasoline-tin stove, we soon had the cabin warm. The dogs we tied under big spruces outside, where they could stay dry, and we had a really comfortable night, the first in the last three or four, in that old cabin.

At six o'clock the next morning we were awakened by rays of sunlight streaming through the cracks between the cabin logs. I opened the door and the room filled with pale yellow light. The sky was clear blue, without a cloud. I wonder if any morning ever looked so good?

A full day's travel brought us to what we called the Whirlpool, one of our most dreaded spots. We had hoped to get it behind us that day, but one look made us decide not to tackle it until morning. We camped on a big, clean gravel bar not more than a hundred yards below. The night was clear. We were all glad of the chance to sleep out and not have to put up the scow cover, but it was getting late enough in the season so that it was quite dark for three or four hours — so dark we could see the stars — and it got pretty snappy during those hours. Elsie dreamed she was driving a dogteam through deep snow.

As we loaded the boats next morning, everyone's eyes were on the whirling, churning water ahead. The Whirlpool got its name from the short turn that shot the fast water straight into the face of the bank, undercutting it and bringing even huge cottonwoods toppling into the current. Some were torn away, roots and all, and rushed down the river. Others hung by their roots, making an even greater hazard, and the water hurled back from the bank created a swift whirlpool that was very hard to navigate. We always talked about it long before we reached it, and we went through it with our hearts in our mouths and felt like cheering the minute we got into the more peaceful water above.

First we had to separate the boats and line the poling boat, full of dogs, up through the old and shallow channel. Then we had to come back, hunting for a place shallow enough to wade so that we could get to the power boats. The water was almost over our hip boots; the current walled up against our hip pockets and almost knocked us down.

The moment we all dreaded came when we had to run the power boats through the whirlpool that seemed waiting to smash to bits against the bank anything that came into it. A big tree already in the water crackled and splashed. We had tied the two boats side by side, for safety in making the short turns, and they heaved and strained at the ropes that held them. With the motors wide open, we moved so slowly that we had to sight on the tree to know that we were making headway. At the elbow kink that formed the whirlpool we were picked up and hurled against the bank three times. Each time we had to cut the motors and drift back to try it again. On the fourth try we made it, but we barely inched forward against the rush of water, and I was holding my breath all the time for fear my engine would conk out as it had a habit of doing at the wrong times. Mother and Hazel, standing with poised poles ready for anything, kept looking back at the engine and I knew what they were thinking. But we kept creeping forward slowly until we were over the worst of the riffle, and then the motors began to shove us along faster and faster. We could hear the dogs howling from the poling boat.

As we headed on up, leaving a silvery V of wake behind, it was hard to believe that at the Whirlpool we had been five hours making a hundred yards.

"Now," Hazel said, "we have only two more dirty places ahead of us." Actually there were several "dirty" places ahead, but only two that were dangerous. The next one we called the Jackpot, because one year we almost lost our whole outfit there.

Usually it took us until noon to get through the Whirlpool, and all that afternoon to get to a campsite just below the Jackpot. Next morning we would be up at five to size it up. The Jackpot consisted of two channels, both crooked, with about equal amounts of water. One channel was swift, with many fallen trees lying along the cutbank and one large birch arching over the narrow channel about six feet above the water. The other was fairly clear of sweepers and not quite so swift, but shallower.

We chose the shallower channel and had no trouble with the power boat or poling boat, and so we thought we could make it with the scow. We tried it: not enough power. There was nothing to do but put on a line. Mom, Elsie, and I were to pull until we came to the head of the island, then Hazel was to throw off the line and go on, leaving us to bring up the poling boat by hand. We were over the riffle when the current caught the front of the scow from the other side, throwing it toward us and the other channel. Hazel threw off the line, but it caught on the side of the boat and pulled it around still more.

I saw what was happening and ran out into the water to try to help straighten her. When I reached her, the boat was drifting crosswise of the current with her propeller hitting the rocks hard. My boots were so heavy with water I couldn't climb in, but had to hang to the gunwale until Hazel could jump across the scow and help me in. By then we were heading straight down the channel and I saw that we were going to hit a tiny island.

Hazel grabbed the rope and yelled "Come on, Evelyn!" just as the bow hit. We both jumped, and as we landed I too grabbed the rope. The scow stopped. The back end began to swing, gathering speed as the current took hold of it. We dug our feet into the gravel and hung on. As our feet dug deeper and deeper into the shifting gravel, our bodies lowered until we were sitting on the beach, up to our knees in gravel and water. By the time the boat swung clear back to the beach and grounded, our hands were so cramped that we could hardly straighten them out. But we had taken a chance on saving the outfit, and succeeded.

The water in that channel was too swift to get up, so that we had to ease the boat down the rest of the way with the rope. Back at our original starting point we took out a poling-boat load and moved it up to the power boat. With the scow lightened, we tried again, and this time we made it.

Another afternoon's run brought us to the big bluff a mile by land and two by river below our home cabin. This bluff was our last dumping place; we always relayed from here to home, making about six trips in the power boat, because there was such a sharp turn, with such a pile-up of water against the bluff, that we couldn't take chances on it. We always camped below the bluff while we went through the long job of relaying; sometimes, if the water was low, we couldn't use the power boat, but had to relay in the poling boat with four dogs on the trackline.

When the relaying was finished, we lined both power boats over the riffle so as to be able to leave them in a small slough just above the big bluff. Then we either swam the dogs across and led them or took them to the cabin in the poling boat, and we were home, ready for another season.

1. LAYING IN SUPPLIES

USUALLY WE ARRIVED at the home cabin about the middle of August, when the berry season was in full swing. The last two weeks of the month we spent picking berries and fishing. If we couldn't get enough berries in the patches nearby, we crossed the river to a big niggerhead flat where there were always plenty. It was about a mile walk from the river, and we always carried a big rifle, just on the chance that something would come up. Nothing serious ever did, but sometimes we did have a little excitement.

Once I was halfway across the flat when I ran onto a good patch of blueberries and got busy picking them. Hazel was somewhere to my left. I heard a twig snap, and the gulping sound she made eating handfuls of berries. This went on for a minute or so, and then I stood up and said, "You should be

IV. Fall Preparations

full pretty soon, Honey Bun, you . . . " I stopped, for what I saw was not Hazel, but a black bear, about fifteen feet away, just rising up on his hind legs.

A little farther away, Hazel said, "Honey Bunch, what?" and then she stopped as short as I had. The bear looked once at each of us and took off across the flat like a black rubber ball bouncing over the niggerheads.

Just then Elsie stood up, right in his path.

The bear rose on his hind legs and fairly turned over, turned at right angles down the flat, and was soon out of sight. I think he was far more scared than we were that time. But we discovered that it paid to keep our eyes open in a berry patch.

When we weren't berrying, we were netting fish for dog

feed, pike and big whitefish in the larger net, and some whitefish, loads of suckers and pike, and a few big grayling in the
smaller one. In late September the grayling came down the
river from the higher creeks for the winter and we caught
them with fly hooks and line, to be frozen for winter use.
At the mouth of Wind Creek, a half mile below home, we
could almost always start fishing at four-thirty in the afternoon and return by seven or eight with all the grayling we
could pack. Just at dusk they bit well, but this lasted only for
a couple of weeks, and in the middle of the hunting season
when we had a lot else to do. On the evenings when we got
to go fishing it was fun to come home with our loads of fish
in the dark. We always had a gun with us, but that didn't
stop us from jumping half out of our skins every time a ruffed
grouse flew up or a rabbit scurried out of the brush or a hoot
owl yelled "Whooooo, whooo!" from a tree right over our
heads. We'd laugh at each other for jumping, but it would
be nice to come out of the dark woods along the dark river
and see the cabin brightly lit and warm. I don't know anything more cheering, when you have been out working after
dark, than a brightly lighted window, and inside the sound
of a radio playing softly. It just seems to call you in.

By the first of September, when the hunting season opened,
the grass was dry enough to cut and store for winter bedding
for the dogs. It usually took us two days to cut enough for
the winter, and on those days we did nothing else. Each of us
took a long butcher knife and a bunch of ropes and a sharp-
ening file or stone with us. The mouths of the sloughs were
ideal places for haying, since they were handy to the boats
and since there were no rosebushes there. We would cut
from nine in the morning till about two, when we would

gather the grass into large bunches and tie each bunch around the middle with a piece of rope and throw it into the boat. By the time the boat was loaded none of it could be seen except the two ends; it was a mountain of dry, light brown grass. As soon as we got it home we fixed each dog a soft bed, and put the rest away for the winter.

Then hunting, a hard three weeks of it, to get enough moose, caribou, and bear to last us through. Generally we hunted upriver in the pole boat. I got my first moose when I was twelve, though I never thought I deserved the credit. Elsie and John and I were hunting in the rain. As we came out of the dripping brush into a niggerhead flat, John stopped and whispered, "Keep still! There's a moose coming over there."

I looked, but couldn't see anything.

Then, as John raised his rifle, I looked where the gun pointed and saw the head and horns of a bull about a hundred yards away. I raised my own .30–.40 Krag, but I was so short I couldn't see well over the brush. John shot, and the moose turned his head. I knew he would start running any second, and so I shot too. To my amazement the moose went down.

John cried, "You got him!"

We heard the brush crashing, and he added, "Come on, he's down, and we don't want him to get up again." When we went over the moose raised his head. John said, "Finish him, he's your moose."

But when I raised my rifle the muzzle went in circles and danced all over. I couldn't even see to line up the sights. "Hurry up!" John said. "Shoot him."

"You shoot him," I said. "I can't see him well from here."

"Step up closer then."

But I said, "You shoot him. I might only scare him and he might get up and run away."

So John shot.

When we skinned the moose we found where John's first bullet had hit, just back of the ribs. My shot had hit the head just under the eye, too low to be a killing shot. John always said I killed that moose. I killed plenty of them later, but I never thought that one was mine.

I remember a trip upriver with John and Hazel, when we camped on the little island at the mouth of the beaver slough. The island was fronted by still, deep water, where tall spruce came right down to the edge of the bank. The other three sides were fringed with willows, and the island was connected to the mainland on both sides by beaver dams. Our tent was set up in the middle, among the spruce, where we could see up and down river. Above camp the water was swift, and it made splashing noises as it rolled over and around roots anchored in the channel.

As we set up camp about five in the evening we could hear the *plink* of grayling jumping for the little white mites that danced along the surface of the still water. With a dry spruce pole and flies Hazel and I caught fourteen big grayling before supper, enough to feed both us and the dogs.

Morning in a camp like that is full of song sparrows and juncos singing in the tops of the trees. The sun streams through the spruce. You feel as if you could jump out of bed and sing with the birds. On that morning I lay in bed an hour, just looking and listening, before Hazel and John woke up and I got out to get breakfast. Just as we finished washing up we heard splashings in the water and the click of hoofs on gravel. Jumping to the tent flap and grabbing for our rifles, we saw a big buck caribou swimming the river. At first we could see only his antlers, like a big snag floating down the river, and then as he reached the shallow water and raised his nose to sniff the air his antlers almost touched his rump. He stopped at the edge to shake off the water; when he was clear out on the bar we shot. Then we went up to look at him. His skin was slick and glossy from the river, and his white neck patch continued well back on his shoulders.

That caribou's heavy skin made a fine mattress for our beds that winter, and the meat was as good as any beef. For that matter, I don't think there is any meat that beats a good fat caribou.

We hunted for about three weeks, usually, until the moose were thin from rutting and the ice began to form in the river. In late September the hills were a maze of red and yellow birch leaves, mingled with the dark green of spruce. The grass along the slough banks turned light brown, and the beaches and bars were lined with yellow leaves that had drifted ashore.

We hunted from the hills, watching from above to spot out moose or caribou. Sometimes we went as far as the boundary of Yukon Territory, a wide slash through the timber reaching on north beyond the Arctic Circle. Up there we found juniper creeping close to the ground, and tried the blue berries that John said were good to eat, but we liked plenty of other things better. Sometimes we walked through patches of low-bush cranberries where the ground was snowed with yellow leaves from the birches, and the green bushes loaded with bright red berries peeped out between them. The ground was so pretty that it made us feel almost ashamed to walk over it. But we walked: we had to have meat.

Once, from the hills, we watched eight big bull caribou walk in single file toward the river, disappear into the spruce that lined the banks, and come out again and look over the bank at the water, running swiftly among trees that had toppled in from the caving bank. The leader tried three times to get down, and at one point they all started to turn back, but the smallest bull came back toward the river on the lope and the others followed. Without a moment's hesitation they all jumped into the foaming water. Some were forced under the sweepers, others swam clear, but after a few seconds of struggling they all untangled themselves and swam across. On our side they shook themselves and started for the hill just above us. As they climbed we started shooting, and we got five of the eight. The last we saw of the remaining three they had swum back across the river and were back where we had first seen them.

Or we had bear troubles. One afternoon we met a moose in the trail and I shot him. We butchered him and went back to camp, to come back bright and early next morning for our meat. One ham was missing. We found it on the other side of a log where a bear had dropped it getting away. On our first trip out with packs of meat we carried Hazel's .30–06 rifle, but a ten-pound gun gets heavy. The next trip we left it by the meat. As John said, if we were going to see Mr. Bear we would see him at that point. He knew where the meat was.

As we came out into the niggerheads where we had left the first load, we stopped to rest. We didn't use sacks to carry the meat, but left the skin on and just strung a rope through cuts in it, using the rope like straps. We had loosened our ropes to take the weight off, and were all resting and each looking a different way, when Hazel said, "Hey! There's that darned bear again!"

A black bear was standing on his hind legs looking at us, one paw resting on a dry spruce pole. As we moved he dropped down out of sight.

John said, "You'll never see *him* again," and settled back against his pack of meat. But as I stood watching to see where the bear went, I saw the brush move, and there was Mr. Bear, much closer than before.

"He's coming nearer," I said.

Hazel picked up a piece of rotten wood and threw it. The bear went over to where it landed, sniffed at it, and then made a half circle around us.

"Shall I go get the rifle?" Hazel asked.

John looked at the bear and then across the niggerheads to where the rifle was, two hundred yards away. "I guess you better," he said. "It looks like he won't go away."

When Hazel started, the bear watched her. Then he settled down behind the brush. I could not see him, but I could hear him walking. Stepping around a big upturned root to look for him, I looked right into his face. He was sneaking up on us from behind the root, and he was only twenty-five feet away. As we faced each other he puffed his lips out and made a blowing noise, went around the other side of the root and circled nearer, blowing as he worked closer with each circle.

Finally Hazel reached us with the rifle. She had run both ways, and was so out of breath she handed the gun to John. John fired at a black spot where the bear was half hidden in the willows, and we heard the willows crashing. John swore and passed Hazel the rifle. "We won't see him again," he said for the second time.

But right then the bear came into sight at the end of an opening. This time his ears were back, his teeth were bared, and he was on the lope straight toward us. Hazel had reloaded her rifle the minute she got it. She fired. The bear turned at right angles and kept going. She fired twice more and he fell. He was as fat as a hog; all three shots had hit him.

The next day when we went back to finish bringing the moose meat to the boat, another ham was gone, and there were new bear tracks, and after a minute Hazel jumped and said, "Look!" and there under a tree was a second black bear. We shot him too and packed his meat out with the other bear and the moose meat before any more bears could come around.

Every morning on the late hunts the ground was white with frost, and for the first hours of morning the river ran slush ice. By the time we would have finished breakfast the frost was melted, and the leaves sparkled with a million drops of water in the sun. I remember a time, a windy day when leaves were blown loose and fluttering to the ground, when we walked through the timber and heard the wind roaring above in the trees. Somewhere among the swaying trees two spruce were rubbing together with loud groaning noises, and when we left one rubbing pair behind us we heard another up ahead.

Then I noticed that the groans were not coming from the spruce at all, but from the cottonwoods along the slough bank, and they went on whether the gusts were thrashing the trees or not. I called Hazel's attention, and we went quietly toward the groaning sounds. They were quite loud when we got to a narrow dry slough.

Hazel whispered, "You stay on this side and watch until I get across, then you come."

As soon as she started up the opposite bank, I followed her. Right at the top I saw her throw up her gun and shoot. I ran across and up the bank just in time to see a bull moose coming straight for us. His eyes were white all around, his horns blotted out most of his huge body. Before I could raise my rifle, Hazel shot again, and the moose hit the ground with a crash that fairly shook the earth.

She had missed the first shot, and when the bull heard the crack of the gun he had charged blindly without looking to see what it was. He was with a cow, and apparently had just driven another bull away and was standing no nonsense. In the length of time it took Hazel to pump another cartridge into the chamber and shoot, he had covered half the distance between the cow and us. While we were standing and laughing at each other for feeling shaky, the cow trotted off into the willows beyond the big cottonwoods.

The next morning when we loaded our meat aboard and started home the ice was running heavy. Ice froze on the trackline until it was stiff and slippery to hang on to. The boat poles were caked in ice. Though the sun shone all day, the shore ice never thawed. The slush in the main stream ran until almost noon.

Those were the signs that hunting was over: rutting moose, freezing river. Unless the hunting had been particularly bad, and the caches were not full enough to carry us through, we put away our rifles for a while and turned wood choppers.

Every fall we had to cut about eight cords of wood. In

the timber about a half mile from the cabin, Hazel and John felled the trees and Mom and I partially limbed them and cut them into sixteen-foot lengths. Elsie limbed all she could while we sawed, and when the felling and cutting were done, Mom and Elsie finished trimming while John, Hazel, and I worked the logs out to the wood road and piled them for loading on the sleds. As soon as there was snow, we loaded and hauled them up to the cabin.

Then there were toboggans to make or repair, dog harness to patch up or replace, traps to get ready, a hundred and one things to do before the trapping season. Our whole life was a preparation for the winters. There were supplies to be sorted out and got ready, campstoves to make out of sheet iron bent into eleven-by-fourteen-inch tubes three feet long, with a door hinged on the front and a hole cut at the back for a stovepipe. All the preparations that started with the buying of supplies in Fort Yukon early in the summer came to a head about the first of November when we set out the traplines. By that time the creek was frozen over, and we generally had four or five inches of snow.

2. SETTING OUT THE LINES

PUTTING OUT lines in the fall was the hardest work of all the trapping season. That was the time when we set out camps and traps, cut new trails and cleared old ones, and killed meat for the out-cabins, if we could find any. If we did find any, we either had to build a cache so it would be handy for use when we ran the lines in winter, or haul it to the nearest cache that was already built.

The first winter we went out alone with John, after Dad went into the hospital, there was an unusually large amount of work to be done, new trails to cut and a cabin to be built. I was twelve and Hazel was thirteen. We went out with John to set out the lines while Elsie stayed home with Mom to do what they could around the home cabin.

John's team had four dogs, Hazel's and mine three each. Because we had to carry supplies for a month, our loads were very heavy. Hazel and I had a terrible time trying to make our dogs keep up with John's. It was early October, and there was very little snow, so that the niggerheads stood up big. We learned to carry a pole for a handspike to pry the toboggans up when they wedged between the niggerheads, for we weren't big enough to lift them as John did his.

It took us a week of wrestling with niggerheads all day and setting up a tent each night before we reached the place where John intended to build a cabin. But before we started building, John said we had to have a moose. He and Hazel left me in the tent while they went hunting each day. Just before dark, when they should be coming back, I would fry up some of the moose meat we had brought from home, warm up a pot of brown beans, make some tea, and bake biscuits in our drum oven, which was a drumlike cylinder fitted on to the stovepipe so that smoke and heat went around through a hollow outer cylinder and out through the stovepipe above, heating the oven on the way. An eight-by-ten baking pan just fitted inside the drum, which was placed about two feet above the stove.

One day Hazel and John did not come at the usual time. I cooked the supper and waited while it grew darker. At six o'clock I fed the dogs. By this time it was black dark. I went back into the tent and blew out the candle so that my eyes would get accustomed to the darkness and I could see farther by the light of the stars. The moon would not be up until later. I felt little and cold and scared, standing out in front of the tent in the thin snow, straining my ears in the quiet for any sound that would let me know they were coming. The northern lights began to wave across the sky like pale red and green silk in a wind, forming on one horizon and rising, growing big and bright across the sky and then fading out as they disappeared behind the dark hill back of the tent. I stood kicking my feet together, waiting and watching the lights, until one of the dogs gave a little bark and stood up and bristled, and I heard John say, "Keep still, boys," and they were back. They had spots of bloody snow on their pants legs and moccasins — a moose, they said, a big one.

With the meat problem taken care of, we could start the real work. Building a cache and hauling the meat to it took two days. Then there were two full weeks of cutting trails, which had to be marked before the snow got any deeper.

By the time we could start work on the cabin, the snow was nine inches deep. While John and Hazel felled trees and laid the first round of the cabin, I took a shovel over to the foot of the hill, shoveled off the snow, and dug out the brown moss for chinking. It had to be thawed in the tent before it could be used. John notched the ends of the logs until the crack was a quarter of an inch to an inch between them. Then Hazel and I covered the lower log with moss and turned the top log over on it. One after another, logs were notched and mossed and rolled into place and the walls went up.

Then came the roof. Two logs were laid lengthwise across

the top of the walls, about three feet apart, and a short log notched into place across each end. A third log was laid across these short logs, parallel to the first two, to form a ridge. Small poles were laid solid from the ridge to the tops of the walls, and these covered with a mat of moss six inches deep. Finally, we chopped through the frozen ground eight or ten inches to find mud to smear over the moss. When the mud was on, the house was finished.

A little out-cabin like this had no windows. The door was a caribou skin with the hair on, tacked over a pole frame and hinged with rawhide. The table was a pole bench eighteen inches wide along one side wall. The bunk, also of poles, was across the back of the cabin. It took up over a third of the house. Under it was piled stovewood. The campstove was in the corner, opposite the table. Green spruce boughs padded the floor and the bunk, and there were a couple dozen nails driven into walls and ridgepoles to hang clothes on and dry them out. That was all there was to the cabin; the whole project took about eight days.

Then there were the dog shelters which we built out of the boughs and tops of the felled trees. In each we made a bed of boughs. That took a couple more days. Our month was up, with not a trap out yet, and no tents set up beyond the cabin or on the sidelines. John said it would be a waste of time to go home without setting out traps, and so for three weeks we were out on the trails we had cut earlier, putting up the tents and setting out sidelines.

We set various kinds and sizes of traps, and in different ways for different animals. Wolf, fox, and wolverine were trapped pretty much alike, and so were marten, mink, and ermine. We had plenty of home uses for other kinds of skins — rabbitskin for lining mittens, caribou hides for cabin doors, un-tanned caribou-hide strips (*babiche*) for mending dog harness and putting tread into snowshoes, caribou or bear skins for mattresses — but the first-named ones were the furs that meant cash.

For wolf, fox, and wolverine we used to trail-set a good deal. First we cut off a tree about four feet from the ground and slipped the chain of the trap over the stump. Then we stood the rest of the tree against the stump to hide the fresh cutting, and set the trap in the trail, preferably at a place where anything coming along would have to step over a down pole and into the trap. A trail set was especially good in thick brush.

Sometimes we took moose or caribou innards and put them in a place where wolves and wolverines frequently passed. We cut a toggle and fastened three or four traps to it, placing them all around the bait, and then we cut hair from a piece of moose or caribou skin and sprinkled it all around thinly so as to cover the traps and a wide area around the bait. Thinking a killing had been made there, the animals would walk right in and get caught.

Often we set steel snares for lynx, fox, or wolves, setting them in the toboggan trails or in the game trails made by caribou and moose which were followed by all the big animals. Sometimes we fastened the snares to a standing tree or willow and hung them out over the trail, and sometimes we fastened them to toggles directly overhead.

Marten, mink, and ermine we trapped differently. Marten are found mostly in the hills that are heavily timbered with small spruce. They have certain places that they travel over time and time again. When the weather is cold, thirty below zero or colder, the marten move to the tops of the hills where it is warmer, and they stay there until the weather breaks. Then they come back down to the foothills and the flats. The best spot to set a trap was right near the bottom of a steep gully, and the next best was the top of a ridge. In country where there were no gullies or ridges we looked for a strip of spruce timber. Even if it was only a narrow strip with just a few trees and with open country on both sides, that was the place for a marten set. Open country was the worst place of all, though I have caught marten in places where the only tree around was the one I cut off to make the set.

Sometimes, on hills completely covered with spruce, a strip of birch trees made a good spot, but not unless we saw marten tracks there. In that kind of country we went entirely by tracks. Where we saw tracks, we set a trap. Because they have to see what everything is, marten are one of the easiest animals to trap. Even a blaze on a tree is often enough to make them come over and investigate.

The usual set for marten, or for mink and ermine, was a small brush pen with the trap in front and the bait at the back. Another that was very good for marten and ermine was what we called our "stump trap." We made it by cutting off a tree a couple of feet above ground, leaving a flat stump. We drove a nail into the top of the stump and bent it over so that the bar of the trap could be slipped under it, thus fastening the trap to the stump. We strapped the chain over the stump and hung the bait with string from a small pole set in the snow so that the small end was directly over the trap. The bait dangled about nine to twelve inches above the trap. A marten coming along and seeing the bait dangling would climb the stump after it and get caught. Ermine got caught a little differently. They climbed the pole after the bait, and then either fell off or jumped off onto the stump, landing on the trap.

Where there was a wolverine working the line and stealing marten, the spring-pole set was very good. We used it either in a house set or a stump trap. For the latter, we tied the spring pole, about twenty feet long, to a standing tree about four feet off the ground. We tied it with rope if there weren't too many squirrels around, with wire if there were, because the squirrels often chewed the rope. We fastened the trap chain to the small end of the spring pole, and pulled it down and hooked it over a headless nail driven into the side of the stump. The trap was set and baited as usual for a stump set. When a marten got caught he pulled the chain off the nail and was yanked into the air when the heavy end of the pole fell down. There he hung six or eight feet off the ground, safe from wolverine, wolf, or squirrel.

Squirrels were one of our worst nuisances. They often cut the fur off a trapped marten and took it down their holes to line their nests. In that part of the world the tree or red squirrels do not live in trees in winter, but dig underground and make big colonies in the spruce timber where they cache spruce cones, mushrooms, and low-bush cranberries for food. They come out aboveground as they wish, but I have seen places where they didn't come out for over a week at a time. Their skins are not worth much now. One winter I skinned over three hundred of them and got thirty cents apiece for the skins.

Wolverine were another matter — even more destructive on a trapline and very hard to catch. There was one wolverine all the trappers around had been after for four years, and never got, that I finally trapped by thinking one step ahead of him. He wouldn't go near a set trap, but if anything was in the trap he would go right up and take it out. He got a big marten from me, also pulled a moose ham off the cache and partially ate it. So I took five traps and fastened them to a tree and pulled the ham over there. I set the traps two in front, one on each side, and one behind the ham. The two in front I set very light so that the Canada jays could easily spring them, and the other three I set as usual. Then I spread moose hair all over the set, covering all the traps except the two in front, which I left uncovered so that jays would be sure to land on them. When I returned two weeks later I had two camp robbers and one big wolverine. My trick had worked as I planned it. Mr. Wolverine had seen the two birds caught and thought everything was safe. He had walked into all three of the other traps, and had one on each front foot and one on a hind foot, and his trap-robbing days were over.

Putting out the lines, we stopped the toboggan and made a set wherever we saw tracks, and wherever we made a set we blazed it. Our trail markers were one blaze on two sides of a tree so that it could be seen from either direction. A trap we marked by two medium blazes on the side of the tree that the set was on. Three small blazes meant a rabbit snare. If we were out of traps and saw marten tracks where we wanted to make a set the next time around, we marked the place with dot blazes. We marked a trail trap by a long blaze on a tree on each side of the trail, fifty yards before we came to the set. That was to remind us not to run the dogs into it, for trail sets were always large traps set for lynx, wolf, and wolverine. They often were toothed, and they were very hard to remove from a dog's foot. Believe me, I know, for I have more than once caught one of my dogs in a trail set.

One time it was my gray and white dog Pinto. He was third in the team that day. The first two got by, but Pinto stepped square on the trap and his whole foot was caught. I stopped the team and rushed up and unsnapped the two lead dogs and tied them to a tree. To relieve the pull on Pinto's foot I also unsnapped his tugs so the back dogs couldn't pull at him. Then came the task of releasing the trap. I couldn't work with my mittens on, for this was a big No. 4 jump trap with teeth in it, and a very stiff spring. When I took hold of the trap Pinto yelped and snapped at my hand. I slapped his face and said, "Stop it, don't bite me now," and he wagged his tail. I put the trap, foot and all on my knee and put my weight on the spring. At first I could get it only halfway down; it took a second try before I got the jaws open. Pinto had his teeth set on my arm. He never moved until I told him, "Take it out, Pinto," and then he lifted his foot and took his teeth off my wrist. There were little blue marks from the teeth, but he hadn't bitten me; he had only been holding on.

We didn't get the traps all out the first winter, and we changed them from time to time, but when our lines were all out and being worked, we had upwards of three hundred miles of trails. At convenient intervals we had cabins, ten of them altogether besides the home cabin, and on the long side-lines and out at the extensions of the main lines we had tents — twelve of them — as shelter camps. Most of the out-cabins had permanent caches for storing meat, and gradually we fixed them all up with campstoves made out of sheet iron.

A lot of our life was spent in those cabins and tents and on those trails during thirteen years. They got to be plenty familiar, but they were never like home.

On that first trip with John, in the fall of 1929, we had been out almost two months before we could start for the home cabin. By that time the caribou herd was moving northward. We could see great bunches of them on the hills and along our trail wherever the timber opened up. Sometimes it seemed as if a whole flat started to move when we neared a large herd. Their towering horns looked like a leafless forest from a distance. Sometimes the herd crossed the trail ahead of the teams, within a hundred yards of us. The woods were alive with them; where they had been feeding on the white caribou moss, the snow was all pawed up. I have never seen so many caribou in all my life as we saw on our way home that trip. The wolves which followed the herd howled night and day.

On the last day we passed up one cabin and made a double run, for we knew that Mother and Elsie would be worrying about our being a month overdue. We pushed the dogs all through the short day and into the early dark, and still we were more than two hours from home. The moon sailed up clear and full, turning the snowy hills to a rich cream color. The trees stood out black and cast long shadows on the snow. If we paused, the only sound we could hear was the howling of timber wolves in the distance. There was not a breath of wind. Overhead the pale green and red northern lights waved as if a gale were whipping them, but on the trail everything was still and cold. The steady scraping of the toboggans on the trail seemed a part of the setting, like the music that goes with a play.

And it was like a picture when we drove into the yard with the house blocked out dark against the snow, white smoke rolling from the stovepipe, warm pink light pouring from the window. Behind it, the moonlight streamed through the tall spruces. The one puppy we had left behind with Elsie barked a welcome, and we were home again.

V. Life on Snowshoes

1. RUNNING THE LINES

I GOT MY INITIATION into the work of running the lines that same winter, about a month after we got back from setting them out. The time between we had spent setting out Mom's lines, all of us working together to get them out fast. When it was time to run them, Hazel and Elsie went with Mom, I went with John.

As we broke camp that morning, the sky was clear, the sun not yet up. The thermometer was near zero. We couldn't have asked for a better day for traveling. Our trail was a sunken shadow covered with eighteen inches of fresh snow. John put on his snowshoes and broke trail while I drove. We had a big load on, but all went well until we hit the first niggerhead flat, where the wind had drifted the snow so that our trail was a high hard ridge. I couldn't hold the heavy toboggan on it; it kept slipping down to one side and burying itself in soft snow. John had to keep coming back to get me on the trail again. Finally I told him he could handle the toboggan so much better than I could that I had better walk ahead.

He laughed. "So you want to break trail! Well, you can try it."

I went on out ahead and kept walking, staying with it until I just had to stop and rest. It seemed to me that I had walked miles. The sun had already started to go down, and the hills were all tipped with pink against the blue of the sky. I thought how nice it would be if I was up there in the sun instead of down in the graying valley.

"Well," John said, "let's get on. We can't rest forever."

I started again, but I couldn't keep my eyes off the high hills. Soon the sun was gone and they were a lifeless cold white again, the same as the snow all around me. In the dusk the trail was the faintest shadow across the snow. By the time we rested again I was dead tired, and everything was dull. Even the sky had lost its brightness, and the cold began to close in from all sides. I asked John how far we had come. He answered, "Oh, about ten miles."

Ten miles. And he had said it was fourteen miles between the two camps. That left four miles to go. I was tired, but that didn't sound too bad.

"Come on," John said. "It'll be dark before we get to the tent if we don't keep moving."

I started again, and I walked and I walked, determined not to rest too soon and show John how tired I was. Finally he called to me to stop and give the dogs a rest. I leaned against a spruce tree and he leaned on the handlebar.

"We don't have too far to go now," he said.

I stood and looked into the distance as if it didn't matter

to me how far it was. My back ached and each snowshoe weighed about ten pounds, but I wouldn't give up. I walked on with my eyes on the tips of my snowshoes, never raising them to look around. I was on the trail, and that was all that mattered. Finally, when it was getting hard to see, I came to a low place where there was water under the snow. I stopped and looked up. About a hundred and fifty feet ahead sat our tent, ice all around it and ice halfway up the walls.

"What's the matter up there?" John said.

"There's water in the trail, and the tent's in it too."

John came up and led the team off to one side to higher ground. He looked things over and said, "It looks as if we'd have to get the tent off the toboggan and set it up on top of the snow."

As soon as we had it up I took the trapping ax and cut spruce boughs to make a floor. John pried the campstove out of the flooded tent with a hooked stick, and set it up in the new tent on two spruce poles. He couldn't go inside the flooded tent without breaking through, for the ice inside was only about half an inch thick. While I unloaded the toboggan and started supper he tried to see what he could do about the flooded tent, and ended up by cutting it off where the ice froze it in.

Supper was fried meat and warmed-up frozen beans, a butter can full of tea, and a thawed-out loaf of bread. Our beds felt good, but it was a half hour before we got them warmed up enough to go to sleep.

The amount of work we had to do on the lines depended on what we caught. We wouldn't have dared take off our mittens to skin anything out on the trail, even if most of the animals we caught hadn't been frozen stiff by the time we picked them up. What we did was to throw them onto the toboggan and take them home to be skinned later. If we caught only small animals such as mink or marten or ermine, or even fox, we had no difficulty, but wolves were harder to handle, and if we had a run of luck we sometimes got loaded down.

On that first trip with John, I was too small to do my share, but as I got older and bigger, and John got weaker, I took over a lot of the work from him. Once in a while I even surprised him. I did it once up on the Stony Fork, just below the Canadian boundary line.

The Stony Fork of the Salmon was a very narrow, swift stream, much swifter than the Salmon itself and carrying over half as much water. Its course was marked by rocky bluffs and steep mountains, and its shores were piled with big rocks. In winter Stony Fork froze to the bottom in many places, so that the water backed up and came over the top of the ice. These places we called "overflows"; we tried to pick our winter crossings where the river didn't overflow very often.

The wolves also picked these places for their crossings, and there were almost always moose and caribou along Stony if there were any anywhere. This made it one of our best wolf-trapping areas. We had three cabins along Stony, although we never used more than two in going over that line. The third we used only when we went up the main river and came home over the low ridges and flats. This last cabin was six miles up the fork, the others twelve and twenty-six.

It was at the farthest cabin, just two miles below the Canadian boundary, that we got most of our wolves. I had several traps set just below the cabin. Shortly before we started over the line on one of our trips we had a big windstorm that drifted the trails badly. I had a lot of trouble with the back team, because by that time John could not handle his toboggan any more, but rode in mine while we trailed his. I had to keep my eye on both toboggans all the time, and where the trail was high or siding it was hard to keep them both coming right. Sometimes I had to go back fifty yards or more to loosen the back toboggan from a tree or put it back on the trail.

By the time we reached the first cabin, twelve miles from home, I felt as if I had done a day's work, but I still had to cut wood, unload the toboggans and turn them over, get snow and melt it for water, make spruce bough beds for eleven dogs, and feed them all. After the outdoor work was done I went inside and rolled out John's bed so that he could lie down, and then I fried meat and heated beans and bread and boiled tea. By the time dinner was over, it was past six o'clock. Then I had to fix a broken string on my snowshoe, and so I soaked *babiche* and went to work by candlelight. I got to bed past eight o'clock.

Next morning I told John to stay home and keep the cabin warm and I would make the round trip to the boundary cabin with one toboggan and eight dogs. John thought he ought to go along and help, for it was fourteen miles to the cabin, twenty-eight round trip. But he finally gave in; he told me I wouldn't have anything to pack back but a couple of wolves anyway.

At my first snare, what should I find but a medium-sized caribou, still alive. I didn't want a caribou, but you can't take a live caribou out of a snare and let him go as I would have liked to do. I did the simplest thing — I shot him and went on to the next trap. That held a big gray wolf. Next I got a cross fox. There were three more sets before I got to the Boundary Cabin, and I found frozen wolves in two of them. With the three wolves and the fox in the toboggan I got back eventually to where I had left the caribou. The wolves, which probably weighed seventy or eighty pounds apiece, I put in the front of the toboggan. The caribou, which went three or four hundred pounds, was more of a problem. I tipped the toboggan on one side and shoved and hauled him in as far as I could. Then I pulled at the toboggan to turn it upright, and the caribou rolled right in. On top of him I put the third wolf and the fox, as well as the ax, gun, and snowshoes.

With that load on I knew that if I ever let the toboggan break off the trail I would never get it back on without unloading, and if I unloaded I might never get the caribou on again. My wheeler, Jack, seemed to know it too, and he worked like a good fellow to hold the toboggan on the trail. So did I. There were some awfully tight places, but we made it to the cabin. For once in my life I was glad to find that the last snare had missed and was drawn up.

As I pulled up, John came out to look. He stared at the mountainous toboggan and said, "How in hell did you get all that in there?"

I just let him wonder. Before I could sit down and talk about it I had to cut more wood, butcher the caribou, feed the dogs, and cook dinner.

Next day we went over the hills to what we called Rice's Cabin on Salmon River, leaving the wolves and caribou at Stony Cabin. We got one wolf at Rice's, and on the way home we got two more, plus one mink and one red fox. The last wolf was still alive in the trap. I had trouble keeping my dogs from piling on him, but I held them with the brake, reached over John for the .22, and shot him while standing on the brake, with the dogs jumping and barking.

That was a pretty good catch, as things went. Sometimes we did very much worse; sometimes we didn't get anything at all for several days on the lines. Once when Mom and Elsie and I were out on Mom's lines we reached the last cabin, six days' traveling from home, without much luck. We hadn't caught a thing for the last two days, not even a marten or an ermine. We had only one sideline to go over before heading back, and I suggested that for that we put all the dogs on one toboggan, with Elsie and Mom riding and me driving, so we would make better time.

"What if we get more than two wolves?" Mom said. "We couldn't get more than two in the toboggan."

"We won't have that much luck," I said. I flopped the toboggan over to empty the snow out of it and scrape the frost off the bottom, and Elsie hooked the dog harness together.

At the first wolf set, trap, toggle, and all were gone. I took the rifle and started off on snowshoes, following the marks where the toggle had been dragged through the snow. In a quarter of a mile I found the wolf, a big black fellow that would have weighed eighty pounds. He was a little more than I wanted to carry that far on snowshoes, so I called to Elsie to send three dogs across to me.

She unhitched the three lead dogs and told Buster, the leader, "Go help Evelyn." They came right along. I tied a dog chain around the wolf's neck and they dragged him back to the trail.

"Well," Mom said, "it looks like our luck is changing. First trap, we get a wolf."

"That'll probably be the only one today," I said.

Two ravens were circling and squealing overhead. Mom looked up and said, "There they are, just waiting for us to leave so they can have their dinner. You better cover that up good or they'll tear half his hide off."

I covered the wolf deeply with snow and then cut down two small spruces and put them on top of him. We went on.

The valley was very narrow. We were very near timberline, and there were only a few spruces among the thick alders. The hills were all bald; little herds of caribou were wandering across the tops of them. The sun shining on the hills made them pink as we walked the last mile, leaving the toboggan behind, to look at the wolf sets in a saddle between two rocky peaks. Elsie took the .22 and I took the .30–.40 Krag. We told the dogs to lie down, and tied the leader.

Halfway up the hill we sat down to rest. The sun felt warm on us, even though it was not warm enough to melt the snow on our parkas. We must have sat for five minutes before Mom said, "You better come back to this world so we can be on our way."

"I wasn't out of this world," I said. "I was just looking at the hills over there."

Elsie said, "Do you know, that sun feels *warm* on my back. I could sit here all day."

"You'd change your mind when the sun went down," I said.

"And it won't be long," Mom added. "Come on, I can

see ravens flying around the hilltop now."

"That's most probably what we've got in our traps up there," I said. "Ravens! They fly into everything."

"I bet we get a wolf!" Mom said. I wouldn't bet her, but I didn't think we would.

At the top we split up to look at the different sets. A couple of minutes later Mom called, "I've got a cross fox."

Elsie called, "I've got a gray wolf."

It was like the Three Bears looking at their porridge. I looked around a minute and called, "I've got to look for my trap. It's gone."

The wind had blown off most of the snow so that I couldn't see where the trap had been dragged. I had got to a big rock fifty yards away, and was starting to climb it to see if I could see anything, when I heard the rattle of the toggle chain. I circled the rock, and there stood a big black wolf.

"Bring the twenty-two over," I called to Elsie. "I've got a black wolf and he's alive."

When we had dragged the now dead wolf back to where the trap had been set, Elsie said, "How are we going to get all these home?"

"If we skin this one we can," I said.

"Won't you freeze your hands?" Mom said.

I told her that the wolf was still warm, and it wouldn't take long. Just the same, during the twenty minutes it took to skin him and reset the trap, the sun sank behind the hill and it seemed to turn ten degrees colder, and my hands, wet with blood and snow, were like chunks of wood.

Mom carried the fox, I dragged the gray wolf, and Elsie carried the black skin down to the toboggan and we started for camp. When we stopped and picked up the wolf we had

buried under the snow the toboggan was so full that Mom
had to hold the fox in her arms.

"What did I tell you?" she said. "Our luck has changed."

"But only for today," I said. "We haven't got any more
sidelines to go over."

We ran the lines every few weeks, depending on the
weather and how far out they were, and we had names for
many of the hills, creeks, and gulches that we traveled over.
Midnight Gulch, Glacier Creek, Windy Valley, Stony Fork,
Wind Creek, Roaring Creek, and the Devil's Washboard were
all on our Salmon River trapline. Roaring Creek got its name
because where our tent stood, although there was ice on the
creek, the swift water underneath was not frozen. It made
a loud, roaring noise as it poured around and over the rocks
under the ice. Midnight Gulch got its name because John
and Hazel went hunting over there one day and didn't get
back until after midnight.

The Devil's Washboard was a terrible piece of country, a
side hill about five miles long with lots of small steep gulches
coming down into the valley. Going over it, you were always
going up and down. Hazel and Mom put in an especially
hard day on it once and didn't get so much as one pelt for
their trouble. They didn't even see any fur sign. When Mom
came into the house she threw her cap and mittens down on
a box in disgust and said, "This is the last time I ever go over
that Devil's Washboard!" From that time on it kept its name.

Most of these names changed as the traplines changed
ownership, but some of them were passed on from trapper to
trapper, and stuck.

There was a kind of law, which nobody ever broke, that if

anyone stopped overnight in someone else's cabin he always left a note saying who he was and what he had taken, if anything. Few trappers ever had writing paper with them, so that the notes were written on scrap paper, wrapping paper, paper sacks, cardboard boxes, even on the margins of magazines or the labels off tin cans, on wooden boxes or fur stretchers. If the writer had no pencil, he sometimes used a .22 cartridge, the lead being soft enough to make faint, clumsy letters. Those were seldom easy to read, but no matter how faint the writing or peculiar the stationery, the letters were always appreciated. Now and then, desperate for anything at all to leave a message on, a visitor would scratch a note in the snow with a stick, but unless the owner came along very soon, the wind and snow would have erased it.

Some trappers kept diaries on the boards of their cabin door or on the hewed sides of cabin logs. They were often very comical, and by reading along over doors and walls and box-board tables we could get a complete account of what the writer had been doing and how much fur he had been getting. Sometimes we got a local name from the writings. On one cabin door that we visited, we found out that the man ahead of us must have sat down in the water and got wet. That was the only explanation for the name he gave the gulch back of the cabin.

All the larger animals — wolf, lynx, and fox — we took on home and threw on the cache to stay frozen until we could get around to skinning them, but the smaller animals we skinned out pretty much as we caught them.

As soon as we got the camp work finished we would bring in what marten, mink, or ermine we had caught (the number of marten usually varied from three to fifteen for a trip), tie a string to the leg of each, and hang them from nails driven into the roof poles of the cabin, where they would thaw out but not get too hot. By the next day they would be thawed enough to skin.

First we ripped the inside of the hind legs from foot to tail, skinned out the legs and tail, and worked the fur loose. Then we ripped the front legs from foot to elbow, took the rear end of the fur and peeled it off over the animal's head, the way someone would pull off a sweater. Still inside out, it was slipped over a long narrow stretcher board pointed at one end to shape the head, which was pulled down tight and tacked in place. Then a spreader stick was slipped under the belly side of the skin — a long, tapered stick that held the pelt tight, but could be slipped out after the skin was almost dry, when the pelt was removed from the board, turned fur side out, and replaced for the final drying. The front legs were held open by two little boards slipped up into the leg holes, so that when the pelt was turned the legs could be turned back through the holes and be on the outside.

When the furs were dry they were tied together with a string run through the eye holes and hung in the cache until time to go to town. Mink, ermine, fox, lynx, wolverines, coyotes, and wolves were all skinned the same way. So were muskrats, though we didn't have to bother so much with a muskrat's head and feet, but could peel the hide off in half a minute or so. Wolves were never brought into the house to thaw, but were thawed outside in the sun, or in a cabin that we used for nothing else. Because wolves are so large, the stretchers we used on their pelts were made of two poles about four inches in diameter, pointed for the head and tied together with wire at the point. On one of the poles we nailed a crossboard, so that when the pelt was stretched and partly tacked down, the poles could be spread apart and the board nailed to the second one to hold them spread. When we wanted to take the skin off, all we had to do was to pull the nail, which let the poles spring back and loosen the stretched skin. Just before they were dry, wolfskins were turned like the smaller skins so that the fur was out.

2. CABIN LIFE

OUR HOME CABIN on Salmon River was sixteen by eighteen. The beds were pole bunks with mattresses on them. There were no closets, no bureaus or drawers. Our clothes hung on nails driven into the walls, or were laid into packing boxes that could be pushed under the bunks. For rugs we had bearskins.

The cabin was kept warm by a small wood range and a heater. Each stove had a stack of wood behind it. For a cupboard we had shelves made of long box boards painted and covered with wrapping paper. Pots and pans hung on the wall. A gasoline lantern hung from the ceiling gave us light.

Normally we ran the traplines every few weeks, but the winter lasted from October to April, and we spent enough time at the main cabin so that it came more and more to seem like home, as snug as a home could be. It got pretty crowded when we washed clothes and had to dry them inside, and with the five of us in the one room the cabin sometimes seemed a little dense, but we liked it and enjoyed it.

The cabin was always full of smells, generally food smells,

because between trips we spent a good deal of time fixing food for trips to the trapline, or to freeze down for later in the winter. We discovered the deep freeze a long time before it got popular in the States, and we didn't have to depend on General Electric for it either.

Our meat was always frozen in big chunks out in the cache. When we brought in a chunk and thawed it out, we cut it into steaks which we laid out on pieces of canvas and froze again. Once they were frozen hard, the steaks could be peeled off the canvas and sacked in clean flour sacks for easy use. The meat that would not make good steaks we ground into hamburger and froze in small patties.

The beans, which were one of our staples on trips to the traplines, were also fixed in advance and frozen for later use. We boiled the brown beans, two or three big pots at a time, and put them into baking pans and froze them. When they were good and hard, we thawed the pans just enough to loosen the cakes of beans, and then broke the cakes into pieces to be packed in flour sacks and kept frozen until needed. Bread, cakes, cookies, doughnuts fried in moose tallow, and sometimes even cranberry, apple, mince, or blueberry pies were also frozen and sacked.

Having everything prepared in advance that way made things very much easier on the trapline trips, where there was always enough to do without a lot of fussy cooking. Every day on the lines, as soon as the fire was going and the dogs were unhitched, we brought in a loaf of bread and whatever other bake stuff we would need that night, and hung the sack on a nail over the stove to thaw. The beans we put in a frying pan with a little grease, covered the pan, and set them on the stove to thaw out and heat. The frozen moose steaks were rolled in flour, put in a cold frying pan with a chunk of grease, covered with a tin plate, and left on the stove until they thawed, when they could be fried. In the out-cabins, in order to leave room on the little stoves for the two frying pans, we always used a clean butter can for a tea-pot, because it could be set back beside the stovepipe, out of the road. We spread our bread with moose grease and cran-berry jam on the lines, but at home we had some butter and different kinds of berry jams and preserves.

Often in the evening in the home cabin we played checkers or knitted or listened to music. Our checkerboard was home-made out of a piece of stiff cardboard lined and colored with a pencil. Checkers were more of a problem, but we solved it by cutting twenty-four quarter-inch pieces off an old broom handle and coloring twelve of them. In the earlier years we had an old phonograph, and I won't ever forget the evenings when we sat or lay around the cabin under the gasoline lantern, which threw a white glare all around and a black shadow straight down. John was usually lying on his bed, reading and smoking. Hazel and Elsie were checker players, Mom and I sewed or knitted.

One evening I was knitting something, and said, "I wish I knew how to knit gloves."

Nobody said anything more about it, but when I got back with John from our next trip, and was picking up my knitting one evening, Hazel, who had never knitted much, said, "Oh, Evelyn, I figured it out."

"You figured out what?" I asked.

"How to knit gloves. If you want, I'll show you how."

She really had figured it out without any instructions at all. From then on, I spent a lot of evenings knitting, until we all had several pairs of warm wool gloves.

Nothing improved our home so much as the radio we got about 1932. We bought an Atwater Kent table model in Fort Yukon and brought it up the river, and almost as soon as we landed and put the winter's outfit in the caches we were busy seeing if we could make it work.

First we went out and cut three of the tallest spruces we could find, each about eight inches at the stump. We hauled them home and set them up about a hundred and fifty feet apart, in a triangle, for the antenna. We were holding our breath as we hooked up the three 45-volt B batteries, one 15-volt C battery, and one 2-volt dry cell and turned the radio on. It didn't seem possible that clear out here on the Arctic Circle, 280 miles by river from the last wilderness town, we could really be in touch with civilization.

It was perfectly still for a minute. Then it hummed, and as we twisted the dial in excitement, music came through clear and silvery as if it were being played just outside. The first station we got was KFI, Los Angeles. The next was New York. The dial could bring us almost any place we wanted.

It took a long time before we lost the habit of jumping up to change the record when a tune stopped playing, and if for any reason we switched off the radio and played the phonograph we came to feel that the phonograph should go on playing indefinitely without being wound or changed. But after the radio came we seldom used the phonograph, for we could get stations all over the world, and get them perfectly, except during a rainstorm.

Our roof had something to do with that, though we could never figure out exactly what. We had covered our dirt roof with flattened-out gasoline cans, and in a heavy rain the house was full of noise. But when we turned the radio on, the noise got ten times worse. Every drop that hit the roof was amplified in the loud-speaker, for some reason.

In the middle of the cabin we had a cellar where we stored potatoes and onions to keep them from freezing. It would have been impossible to dig the hole deep enough to be safe from frost, so we piled the sacks of things that we wanted to keep thawed in the middle of the cellar and covered them with all the extra bedding we had. In the corner we put a lighted coal-oil lantern with the flame turned low. The lantern would burn for a week or more, giving a small but steady warmth. I have kept things thawed for two weeks or more that way. We never had to bother with it much after Christmas, because our potatoes were always gone by that time. But once we had the radio we used the system in another way, and stored the battery in the cellar with the lantern every time we left the house for any length of time.

On trips to the traplines we generally broke into two groups, Hazel, Mom, and Elsie going one way and John and I the other. Once, when the others were a day or so behind us getting home, Hazel came in from taking care of the dogs carrying a cardboard box and calling to Elsie over her shoulder to bring the rabbit leg. She set the box on the floor and opened it to reveal a little red fox.

When she held the rabbit leg out, the fox sniffed it and started eating. She let it finish the whole leg before she lifted it out of the box. She had caught it in a wolf trap, and since its fur was worthless, had brought it home to make a pet of. Its leg was broken from the trap, and the mangled flesh was frozen. With her pocket knife Hazel cut off the broken and frozen leg, and then she bandaged the stump with clean cloths. She kept the fox in the tent and fed it on rabbits each day. The leg was badly inflamed, and after a day or two the frozen flesh began to slough off, so that we had to change the bandage three times daily for the first ten days.

Through all this the fox was very gentle and never tried to bite us. Sometimes as we worked on her she licked our hands. We had a hard time to keep the wound healing, but after two weeks, when we had to go over the traplines, it seemed to be getting well.

Mom, who stayed at home that trip, was likely to sit and read or sew for hours at a time without making a sound. Apparently the fox got very wild because of this; if Mom moved suddenly or came near the box where the fox was kept, it would growl and snap at her. But if the radio were playing and noise going on, it would lie down and sleep.

Four days after Hazel and Elsie had left, I came back from my trip and found the bandage dirty and falling off. When I asked Mom why she hadn't taken care of it, she said she couldn't do a thing with that hateful little fox, and if I tried I would get myself bitten.

I walked over to the fox and said, "How about getting fixed up?"

The fox lay over on one side and held up a front leg and a hind leg, and I reached down and rubbed her side and found her as gentle as ever. I washed the leg with warm water and soap, and put salve and a new bandage on it, and she made no move to bite me. But Mom didn't trust her.

Later, when it was getting toward the end of winter, along about the end of March, the fox's leg was entirely healed, and she was fat and slick and full of life. On nights when the moon shone through the window she jumped around all night and made so much stir that Mom made us move her outdoors to a small kennel we had built for a pup the previous fall. Hazel made her a leather collar which fastened with a buckle; we tied her with a light dog chain, the snaps wired so that she couldn't get loose.

The fox belonged to Hazel, and Hazel was supposed to take care of her, but sometimes Hazel was gone. One day when I had just finished feeding the dogs Mom asked me if I had fed the fox, and I said no, I had forgotten the darned fox. Mom jumped up impatiently and said something about the fox being a nuisance, and went to feed her.

Next morning when Hazel and Elsie got in, Hazel said, "How's the fox?"

"Fat and sassy," I said. "All healed up. Mom has her tied up across the ditch."

Hazel and Elsie went over to see her. In a minute they yelled, "She's not here!"

I went over. The chain lay across the top of the kennel, the collar unbuckled and hanging from its end. No one ever knew how she had got loose, but we thought we could guess.

We never saw her again, but she didn't go far away from the cabin, for we found her three-legged tracks all over. Once we even found where she had killed a Canada goose, and so we were pretty sure she wouldn't starve.

That was the only pet, except for our dogs, who were really working animals, that we had in the thirteen years we spent on the Salmon. But we couldn't blame Mom, even if Mom had probably turned the fox loose. She had plenty to think about without being bothered by a fox. We all admired Mom. She was only five-feet-three, and she weighed then about 150 pounds, though later she shrank a good deal. She was a very pretty woman, with sky-blue eyes and almost black hair. I can still remember how pretty she looked, as she came off the muskrat lakes on the Sheenjack when I was a little girl, with her cheeks all pink from the cold and wind and her eyes full of light. She was sometimes discouraged, but she never gave up for a minute. She was always working: If she wasn't out on the trail or cutting wood, she was cleaning the cabin, baking bread, washing clothes, mending, knitting, or sewing moccasins for us. When we were small she often played games with us on days when we couldn't play outside. She showed us all the indoor games she knew — Musical Chairs, The Farmer in the Dell, Drop the Handkerchief, In and Out the Windows, and many others that I have since forgotten. And she often sang to us. I imagine I know more songs of her day than any person of my age alive, and I learned them all from her.

It never entered our heads to question how she treated us, or how John treated us. We never stopped to think what was girl's work and what was men's work. It was all work, and if it needed to be done, we had to do it. Mom set us an example that way by never shirking any job, however hard or dirty, herself.

3. DOGS

THE SEVEN DOGS we had started with in 1929 were added to, as we girls got older, and in the summer of 1932 we bought a bitch named Wolf so that we could raise our own dogs. On July 2, while we were camped on a mosquito-infested bar near the mouth of the Salmon, she had nine pups. Eight were gray. One — mine — was black. She was the runt of the litter, weighing less than a pound, and she was part police dog and part Husky and part a lot of other things that we never knew about, but she was my dog. I named her Katy.

When it was cold and rainy I often tucked her inside my sweater and sat by the campfire to warm her shivering little body. Before her eyes were open she had her name, and as she grew we used to play together, Katy tugging and chewing at my hair and growling at my ears.

She was special from the time she was a pup. One chill rainy morning when Hazel got out to start a fire, Katy came out sniffing and growling from behind the grub box. As Hazel said, she didn't have teeth enough to hurt anything, but she was guarding that grub box and sounding fierce enough to scare a bear out of his skin.

One day when she was about two months old, and we had got back to the home cabin, I couldn't find her anywhere. I called and called. The other pups came, but no Katy. Then Elsie said she had seen Katy a little while earlier by the woodpile. This was a stack of sixteen-foot logs corded up against two posts at the end of the shed. At the wall of the shed it was about seven feet high, sloping away to the ground within about ten feet. I climbed up and looked down between the woodpile and the wall, where the posts held the logs out and left a space about six inches wide. There was Katy, wedged in between wood and wall. Every time she moved she wedged herself tighter.

We tried hooking a forked stick under her collar and pulling her out, but had no luck. Eventually we had to tear the whole pile of logs down to get her. She was limp and apparently dead by that time, but in a minute she revived and was on her feet again.

The three pups that we kept got their first training to harness that fall. One day as we were calling them for their lesson, Lad and Dan came running with their ears and tails down. They kept looking back.

"Where's Kit-Kat?" Hazel said.

The pups whined and looked back. "Well," Hazel said, "let's go get her."

They started off, and in five minutes Hazel was back with Katy in her arms and the other two jumping around. "Something's always happening to this poor little devil," she said. A stick the size of a lead pencil had run through her foot. It had not broken through on top, but poked up the skin in a big lump. She stayed in the house the rest of that day, but in another day or so she was back in the harness with the others, starting her life work as a sled dog. They were three good pups; by the time they were six months old they were pulling a light toboggan by themselves, behind the team of older dogs.

Sometimes Katy was in the lead, sometimes Lad, but when they were sixteen months old I started training Katy seriously to lead a team of five dogs. She was so playful that it took some time to teach her not to run off the trail on every track. But she was quick as a flash, quicker than any of the others, and everything was like play to her. At the end of that trapping season she was already a leader, though she wasn't yet two. She knew "Gee" and "Haw" and was pretty good at following trails. Now that she was full-grown, she weighed forty-eight pounds; if she stood on her hind feet she could put her front paws on my chest. Actually she was barely more than half the size of her brothers, but she did a dog's work. She had already broken more than a hundred miles of trail, and she knew that she was supposed to stay on the trail no matter what happened. Though I had two other leaders, neither was as good as Katy.

One day Elsie and I were going over a sideline. It had snowed two feet since anyone had used the trail. The blazes were all covered, and the white bumps of the marten trap houses looked like any other white bumps. Katy was in the team, third dog back, as she had been when we cut that trail weeks before. I walked ahead until I could no longer follow the trail at all. Then I tried putting Katy out ahead as a loose leader and snowshoed behind her, letting the team come on after me.

She was plowing snow so deep and loose that it fell in on her back; at times all I could see was her head, like a beaver's head at the point of his wake. But she led us right along. After a couple of miles I thought I would rest her. I put Happy on, but the moment I said "All right," he crawled in under a spreading spruce tree and lay down where the snow was shallow. No matter how I coaxed, he wouldn't come out. I finally had to go in and drag him out. He wouldn't go ahead on the trail, and kept crawling under trees, until in disgust I put him back in the team and took Katy out.

"Okay, Katy, go ahead," I said.

With one big jump she was past me into the loose snow. She plowed on for a quarter of a mile, and then stopped and looked at a bump beside the trail. When I went over and stepped on the bump with my snowshoe, I saw the cut ends of the sticks that formed a marten house. With my snowshoe as a shovel, I dug the trap out, rebuilt the house, and reset the trap. After that, Katy stopped at every set on that trail and lay down in the snow with her nose pointed toward the bump that was the trap house. More than once Elsie called, "Are you sure she's on the trail? I don't remember this place."

But she was on, all right. She knew better than we did.

When we came to the end of that sideline, Katy's eyes were full of water and the snow sifting through her fur had formed ice-balls all along her back from her tail to her ears. "That little runt is about played out," Elsie said. "We've got lots of dog power, with ten in the team. Let's let her run loose behind the toboggan."

We put Jerry in the lead, but he poked along. All the dogs looked back, and wouldn't pull. We changed to Happy, but he was worse. I was sweaty and chilled and got tired of fooling around, so I put Katy on again. That was what they wanted. Their tails came up and they pulled like good fellows. We were kept busy dodging trees as we went up and down over a series of small ridges. By that time it was dark; we had only stars to light our way home. But Katy led us back in two and a half hours over a trail that we had been eight hours in breaking, coming out. That was just one of many times she saved the day with her faithfulness and her smartness in following snowed-out trails.

She was like her police dog ancestors — faithful to one master, which was me. She often slept under the bunk inside the little out-cabins while the other dogs slept in their shelters outside. In the team she paid no attention to the commands of others, but the slightest whistle from me and she was in the collar. Other members of the family could drive her if I first told her to go and mind them, but if they put her in the team and I hadn't told her to mind, she wouldn't pull.

The only way I could keep her from working too hard was

to turn her loose behind the team now and then, for if she was in the harness she never stopped pulling. One day I was handling the toboggan and John was snowshoeing behind. He was old and didn't walk very fast, and soon we got a long way ahead of him. When I stopped in the trail to wait for him, Katy jumped up on me to be petted, and kept looking back and whining.

"All right," I said. "Go back and get him, then."

She ran a little way and stopped.

"Go on," I said. "I'll wait."

Off she went. In about five minutes I heard John say, "Oh, go ahead!" Then he swore and said, "Well, stay behind then."

Soon he came into sight with Katy right behind him. As he came up he said, "What's the matter with this dog? Did you whip her? She won't go ahead of me. She just lay down and whined until I passed her, and then she came along."

"I told her to go back and get you," I said.

John looked at her and said, "Well, she did. She walked all over my snowshoes trying to make me get along faster."

Katy jumped up and licked my face, and I patted her and told her she was a good dog. Right away she went around behind John again. She was going to make sure he didn't get behind. But I told her it was all right now, and put her back in the team.

John and I had three ten-day traplines. We decided that two of them could be connected very easily, and that we could save three or four days of travel by doing so. The sideline from the Boundary Cabin on Stony Fork would have to be lengthened to connect with the side line from Rice's Cabin on the Salmon River. That meant cutting three or four miles of trail.

We left Boundary Cabin at about eight, which in that season, November, was before daylight. John had five dogs, I six. Katy followed the trail until we came to the end of the sideline, where she stopped. Then I took the trapping ax and snowshoed ahead. The hill was thickly timbered with small spruce and alder brush. It was nearly a mile to the top of the divide. John was about sixty-eight years old, and none too good on snowshoes in thick brush any more. Whenever my toboggan hung up on a tree or bush I had to walk back and loosen it and then go ahead again. It seemed to me that all I did was walk back and loosen the team, and we didn't reach the top of the divide until about three in the afternoon, when it was already beginning to get dark.

From the top of the divide we could see the Salmon River beyond the rolling foothills, and the steep white hills, almost bluffs, beyond it. The international boundary line lay like a wide white ribbon over the dark, timbered hills, fading out at timberline and beginning again in the next valley.

We had to go around the sidehill a little way before dropping down into the valley where the other sideline ended. The alders were thicker than ever. Going down I had the same trouble I had had going up, only more of it. After I had cut a stretch of trail I had to come back and get the toboggan and drive it down, braking with my snowshoes to keep the toboggan from running over the dogs. The valley bottom was a network of alders of all sizes, from small switches to trunks two inches through. By now it was gloomy-dark in the valley, with the cold moonlight just touching the tops of the hills around us. Somehow I felt that if we could only get through into the moonlight, everything would be easier.

We worked our way down the valley and after what seemed hours we came to the trail leading on to Rice Cabin. I told Katy to go ahead, but before long she began to hesitate and whine, and I remembered that she had never been out this far on the Rice Cabin trail, and that it was two years since she had been out even partway. Happy, my other leader, had been out this far. I put him on and he led us right, but the dogs by now were getting tired, and one or two of them were not working. They poked along at a slow walk until we hit the end of the sideline trail and struck the main one, and then they speeded up a little. Actually they were only going about two miles an hour, but John couldn't keep up. He grumbled something about running the legs off my dogs.

I was a little mad, because my dogs were bucking eight inches of new snow and his were walking in my snowshoe tracks. It took only two of them to pull his load, and so I told him if he couldn't keep up to take off his snowshoes and ride. But by then *he* was mad, and he yelled, "Oh, go on! It don't matter about me anyway."

I went ahead a hundred yards and had to stop and wait again. When he caught up with me he hollered, "If you're in such a darn hurry, go on to camp. If I can't make it I'll lie down by the trail till morning."

Again I told him to take off his snowshoes and ride, but no, he was going to walk. So I sat down on the handlebars of my toboggan and waited some more, while he carried on about how he was too old to be any use any more, and how I would save grub if he froze to death.

I repeated, "Take off your snowshoes and ride. You've got plenty of dog power to pull you."

He still refused. I sat down, thinking that the dogs could

use the rest anyway. Now we were in the moonlight and I
felt better; it seemed as though the work was over, although
we still had six miles to go.

After a few minutes John roared, "ARE you going to sit
there all night?"

"Yes," I said, "if you don't take off your snowshoes and
ride."

We were silent for a few minutes more. The moonlight
fell cold and still all around us and made tangles of black
shadows among the alders. After a while John said mildly,
"Well, go on!"

I asked if he had taken his snowshoes off. He had, and
would try riding for a while. But he wouldn't try to hold on,
and so of course he fell off. He began to swear and protest
that he couldn't hang on to the thing, but I had been watching
him. I had seen him let himself fall off. So I said, "You could
if you wanted to — or tried to."

John got up again, and that time he stayed up.

The moon was perfectly round, and the sky was bright
with stars. The little spruces stood out in the light as though
each owned the entire flat it stood on. The dogs' tails were
high, and I felt as though nothing mattered. Even getting to
the cabin held no interest, for the hill and the valley and the
moonlight and everything seemed to belong to me alone.

We crossed a deep creek, and when my team had dragged
the toboggan up over the bank I left them and went back to
help John. When we got his team to the top, mine was gone.
I called, "Whoa, Katy! Whoa, Happy!" and snowshoed on
ahead. About two hundred yards down the trail I saw them
waiting for me with their ears pricked up as if they had heard
something down the river.

I stopped and listened too. In the distance I heard the low howl of a timber wolf, and then the answer of a pack farther on. They belonged to the night, as we did.

We left the flat and went into the big spruce timber for half a mile. In the last stretch before the cabin, John fell three or four times, and I had to go back and help him up. It was twelve o'clock, midnight, when we finally made the cabin. We had been mushing for sixteen hours through the hardest kind of going.

Or maybe not the hardest. Going back from that same trip we had a taste of another kind.

We finished running the lines and started back toward the home cabin, five days' travel away, on Christmas Day. It was bright and sunny when we left, and everything was covered with six inches of pure new snow. The little log cabin in which we had spent the night looked as if it had been taken from a Christmas card, with the green spruces all around it drooping with fresh snow and the gray smoke rolling up against the clearness of the sky. The sun tipped the hills with pink. We had waited for the sun to shine on the hilltops on purpose — waited until eleven o'clock — because it was 40° below zero.

Just before dark we reached Basin Cabin, built on a hillside. Both of us were stiff with cold; my fingers turned white as I unstrapped the dog harness and unhitched the dogs. As I carried loads from the toboggan into the cabin I looked at the thermometer on the wall. It was 54° below zero now. A fire, and a snug cabin, never felt better.

All night we were perfectly comfortable, but when I opened the caribou-skin door in the morning, the cabin filled instantly with thick white steam. I scrambled out and looked at the thermometer. It was 78° below zero. The dogs were white with frost from their own breathing, and each was steaming like a pan of hot water. With my ears stinging after only two or three seconds, I crawled back through the two-by-two-and-one-half door, yelling, "Seventy-eight below, and that's *cold!*"

There was no choice. We had to go on, for we had only three nights' dog feed left and that was just enough to get us home, with four days and three nights on the trail. We put on our heaviest clothing and started out. A cloud of white steam moved with us. In the intense cold caribou and moose could be picked out easily by the steam that hung over them. Every little stick that broke sounded like the report of a .22. The snow was like sand that ground and swished against the toboggan. The dogs were white as ghosts, and the fur of our parka hoods was encircled with frost. We both had to walk all the time to keep from freezing.

The cabins were cold for hours after we got the fires going, and every time we opened the door to go out we got a shower of frost on our heads. When we set a five-gallon gasoline can on the stove to melt snow for water, it steamed instantly, as though it were hot. Any water spilled on the dirt floor froze, and stayed frozen. Water in the water cans froze solid inside the cabin at night, and the cans popped like gunshots when we put them on the fire to thaw.

On the fourth day we saw the smoke of our home cabin, and as we got nearer, there were Hazel and Elsie sawing wood to beat the band. They were working so hard they didn't hear us coming, but when they did they came on the run to unhitch our teams, and told us to get in and warm up while they cared for the dogs. Mom had made a pot of hot tea, and had bread and butter ready. We took a big breath and loosened our heavy clothes and pulled the ice-crusted parkas off our heads and sat down.

Our thermometer had been right in recording seventy-eight below. It was still seventy-eight below.

Our dogs worked well on that cold trip home. Sometimes weather that wasn't half as cold, or wasn't cold at all, bothered them more. I remember a time in 1938 when we were coming back from the first trip of the season over the lines. It was November, and the weather was clear and cold, but on the next to last day before we reached home, the wind came up strong from the southwest. Such a wind always meant storms. We broke camp early, for we had fifteen miles to go to the next cabin.

By the time we were half way, and into a considerable open stretch, it was snowing hard, the flakes driving before a wind so strong we could hardly face it. If we looked up, the driving snow stung our eyes shut. We could not see a hundred yards ahead. The dogs wore balls of ice all over their heads. Crossing the open flats we were chilled by the cold wind, but in the timber again we warmed up quickly. Then as we crossed the next flat the wind, though still strong, seemed warmer.

It was. Within minutes, a chinook was upon us. Big fluffy flakes, too heavy for the wind to blow away, stuck where they fell. As we traveled on, the wind lessened and finally stopped altogether, but the wet snow continued to fall. As it slacked off, rain took its place, then snow mixed with rain.

Underfoot the snow was sloppy and wet for an inch below the surface. It balled up on the toboggans and the feet of the dogs. Water dripped from the dogs' fur and from our jackets. We were all wet through. The toboggans slipped easily on the sloppy snow.

About a half mile from camp we came to a place where the trail was high with drifted snow, and each toboggan slipped a little to the downhill side. Mine slipped clear off and buried itself in the soft snow. The dogs stopped. I worked and worked, but I couldn't move the toboggan. Even when Hazel took her team off and hooked them on ahead of mine, and we both heaved, with twelve dogs pulling, we couldn't budge it.

Eventually we cut poles and pried the toboggan up. For its full length there was a wad of snow a foot thick stuck along its bottom. It took us twenty minutes with two axes to scrape it off and get the bottom slick enough so that the dogs could pull it.

The snow was cold under the thin layer of sloppy slush on top, and the minute the toboggan touched it it had frozen on.

Hazel never did let me forget that. She said, "I always knew your poky dogs were no good, but I never thought they'd go so slow they'd freeze down!"

4. WOLVES

I HAVE OFTEN heard people say that wolves will not attack a human being, but my sisters and I had at least two experiences that made us think otherwise. One happened in 1932, the other five years later.

The first one was in February, during the caribou migration, one of those bright winter days when the spruce seemed to have turned greener and the sun was bright on the snow. A flock of ravens, as Mom and Elsie and I came in from a sideline, were diving and yelling down on something in the flat below us, and we knew that there must be a wolf killing down there. Camp robbers fluttered on every tree. On the low ridge ahead a herd of caribou were pawing at the white moss, their hides glossy in the sunlight. Off to our right another herd came single file along a well-beaten trail. They did not see us, but they stopped with their heads up to listen. I took off my beaver cap so that I could hear anything they did.

Far off beyond I heard a band of wolves howling. Then ahead of us I heard another band, closer. The dogs stood very still, their ears up, listening.

The caribou in the trail turned around and went back the way they had come. The herd on the ridge put up their ears, looked around, and resumed their pawing, but when we started our teams they ran up the ridge to our left. As we traveled on toward home we passed six different caribou killed and partly eaten by the wolves, and when we reached our little cabin on the hillside we could hear bands of wolves all around us, though faint and far away.

I wanted to build a new sled and had but one birch runner. When we had fixed the camp and cared for the dogs it was only two o'clock, and the sun was still bright. Elsie and I took an ax and went up the hill behind the cabin in search of a good birch tree. Along the thickly wooded slope we waded without snowshoes, playing we were two caribou in deep snow. I was fifteen and Elsie twelve; we still played a lot of games as we worked.

I said, "I hope those wolves don't come and eat us up."

Elsie let out a long howl and galloped toward me. "I'm a wolf!"

"Then I can't stay a caribou," I said. "Caribou and wolves don't stay together."

We got wallowing around in the snow on all fours, howling at each other, and the wolves answered from somewhere on over the hill. Then we couldn't get any answering howls out of them; they had all stopped. "We must have said the wrong thing to them," I said.

From down below we heard Mom calling us to come and eat, and we ran and fell and rolled down the hill to the cabin. "Look at you kids!" Mom said. "Take off your outside things and shake the snow off. Hurry! Dinner's waiting."

As we were going in again after shaking the snow off, we heard one of the dogs bark and then growl. They were looking up the hill where we had been. Elsie and Mom and I stood in front of the cabin and looked where the dogs were looking. It was utterly still. "Do you realize that this is the first time all day we haven't been hearing two or three bands of wolves?" Mom said.

"If you want to hear some wolves, I'll start some howling for you," I said. I howled, and Elsie howled.

We had hardly closed our mouths before the wolves started, and they were very close. The dogs growled, and the hair on their backs stood on end. Elsie looked at me, and I knew what she meant. The wolves were right up where we had been five minutes before.

Their howls had hardly died away before another pack started. All that evening we could hear them from every direction, while the pack on the hill stayed where they were. We didn't have to go outside to hear those.

Just before we turned in for the night, we all stepped outside for a moment, and Mom said, "What a beautiful night!"

The rising moon looked like a red ball on the hilltop; it made a long shadow from every little tree. The northern lights waved in bands of pale red and green across a sky studded with stars. The North Star was almost straight up above the cabin, and the Big Dipper was easy to find. We were admiring the night, so cold and still and polished, when the most awful howling started up right next to us. The dogs leaped up as though they had springs under them, and I grabbed the rifle that always stood by the door.

"Fire a shot toward them and see what happens," Mom said.

But I was hoping that we would see one, so I said, "If we yell 'Shut up!' at them they'll go away."

Elsie and I both yelled, and the wolves stopped howling. "See?" I said. The dogs lay down again and all was silent. "Go to bed, dogs," I said, and "Watch them, dogs," Mom said.

As we went in to go to bed, Mom said, "I'd hate to be a poor caribou tonight." For a while we sat on the bunks, and she told us stories of how the wolves in Russia killed people. Every once in a while the dogs started howling again and we went outside and shut them up.

About nine o'clock the pack was so close that the dogs whined and growled and wouldn't shut up. As I got off the bunk to go outside, the three tied behind the cabin started to yell as though they were being killed. I rushed out with the .30–.40 rifle and ran around to where I could see the dog shelters. All three were lying flat on the snow, as near the cabin as their chains would let them go, and all were growling softly. "Pete, Dick, Jerry, shut up!" I said.

They looked at me and whined. Then Candy, tied about thirty feet in front of the house, let out a yell. I whirled around and said, louder than I intended, "What the hell was that?"

I heard a wolf running through the snow. The hillside was so thickly grown with small spruce trees that even in the bright moonlight it was impossible to see him.

Mom said, "If you want to keep that sugar-coated mutt of yours you'd better move him closer to the house tonight."

I turned to Elsie and said, "Go down and get Candy while I stand guard over you."

Elsie retorted, "Why don't *you* get him? Give me the gun and I'll keep you covered. And don't make a false move."

"Do I have to keep my hands up?"

We all laughed. I gave her the gun and went down and untied Candy. I could hear the wolves jumping through the snow, and as soon as I unsnapped his chain he started pulling for the cabin so hard it was all I could do to hold him. We tied all seven dogs so close that we could cover any one of them from the door. For a while we stood listening to the wolves howl.

"Why don't you fire a shot with your Krag and scare them away so we can get some sleep?" Mom asked.

I fired, and we heard the wolves running through the brush. "That should settle them for the night," Mom said.

We went to bed, but from time to time the dogs howled and we yelled at them to shut up. About eleven-thirty a loud howling awakened us, and Mom said, "Darn those dogs. Go out and whip them before they call the wolves back again."

I stepped outside. The dogs were not making a sound. The

howling was all from the wolves, and they were all around the cabin.

Mom came to the door. "Listen," I said. "They'll all shut up if I yell."

I screamed, and they all stopped howling.

"You sounded as if you were being killed," Elsie said.

Then all at once all the wolves in the world were howling, right on top of us. I threw a shell into the chamber of my gun, and Mom said, "Fire a shot, quick. Those are too close for comfort. If you're going to scream as if you were half dead they'll be in here to finish the job."

I fired. Some wolves barked, some whined, but they all ran. I could hear them lunging through the snow, and I fired again just for luck.

The rest of the night was quiet, but when we went out and looked around the next morning the snow was trampled and tracked in every direction. There must have been fifty wolves around the cabin. It would have been a good time to see whether they really would attack a human, but we were just as glad we had stayed inside the log walls of the house.

The second experience, in 1937, with a pack of wolves was even more convincing to us. One day about midwinter Elsie and Hazel were going over a sideline up a small creek called Cache Creek because the Boundary Survey had built one of its caches on an island in Stony Fork near the mouth of the Creek. The girls were nearly at the end of the line, where the trail ran along the foot of the green spruce-covered hills. Across the narrow creek were more hills, very steep, with small rocky bluffs where the river swung against them. Along the creek itself, spruce and alders were so thick that it was impossible to see more than a few feet. There were many places where caribou had pawed up the snow looking for the white caribou moss that covered the ground under the two-foot snow blanket.

They were moving steadily along the trail, when the dogs put their ears up and started to run. Elsie and Hazel thought they were chasing a caribou, and though they did not want to kill any caribou, they did want to get over the line as fast as possible and return to the cabin, and so they urged the dogs on.

The team was almost loping when a huge gray wolf appeared in the trail, coming toward them. Elsie, driving, stepped on the brakes and yelled, "Whoa!"

The team came to a stop, but the wolf did not. Two or three more appeared out of the brush-obscured trail behind him. Then the woods were suddenly alive with wolves on every side, closing in on the team.

The gun was in the toboggan under the traps, bait, and snowshoes. Hazel dug for it as the wolves closed in. Some of them were pups, not yet a year old, and they were afraid, but the older wolves had no fear at all, and were obviously coming in for the kill. One of the dogs snapped the fur under a big wolf's chin and the wolf skipped around but came on.

Elsie, hearing a sound behind her, looked back. Not more than twelve feet back on the trail a gray wolf was sneaking up on her. "Hazel!" she said, "get that gun quick!"

Hazel passed her the gun and she pumped in a shell and shot without taking aim. The shot broke the wolf's shoulder, and he disappeared into the brush. He had barely disappeared when another came up the trail from the rear, coming right

Mom, Elsie,
John, Hazel,
and Evelyn
at home

Hazel and
Elsie track-
lining the
boat up
Salmon River
with Punch,
Katy, and
Prince

A summer
camp on
Black River.
Mom, John,
Elsie, Evelyn,
Pete

Evelyn, aged 12, with
the head of her first moose

The girls and
netted salmon

Hazel and Elsie
with hunting snowshoes

Elsie and
grizzly

Mom in
toboggan

Meat cache

John digging out
winter tent camp

Elsie's team

Bill O'Brien at his home cabin

Evelyn
and wolves

Evelyn and Hazel
skinning and stretching
wolves

Top row: coyote,
fox, and a wolf at
the right; left and
bottom: marten,
ermine, and mink

in on the lope. Elsie dropped him just nine feet from the toboggan.

The two shots scared the rest of the pack off for the time, and they disappeared back into the brush. The girls did not follow the wounded one: they had only the one gun, and if they left the dogs the wolves would close in and kill them. So they picked up the one dead wolf, turned the team around, and got back to the cabin as fast as they could. The pack followed them, howling and barking but keeping just out of sight, almost all the way.

1. ACCIDENT ON THE TRAPLINE

THE END OF the winter season had its own special feel and it was exciting to come to the door some morning and feel the mild air of the first thawing weather in your face, and as the breakup continued, to hear the melted water running under the snow, and finally to watch the ice break up and come grinding down the river on the floods. If we had had a good catch, we looked forward to the breakup, and the trip downriver, and Fort Yukon, but if the catch had been poor, we wanted spring to hold off a little longer. And we always had a round of spring jobs to do.

When the trapping season was over, we had to run all the lines and bring in the tents and the camp stoves and traps for use the next year. Then we had to skin and stretch the pelts of all the larger animals that had been kept frozen on the

VI. End of the Season

cache. As rapidly as we could handle them, the wolves, lynx, and fox were brought into the old cabin, otherwise unused, and thawed, skinned, and stretched. Next we had to cut and dry any meat left over from our winter supply, for it would spoil rapidly if allowed to thaw on the cache, and we needed the dried meat during the summer when we could not get fresh.

There were no muskrat lakes on the Salmon, and therefore no ratting season in the spring, but about the middle of May, when we had all the other chores done, we started trapping beaver. Actually the season opened on April first, but we didn't start trapping until the ice went out, when we could put the power boat in the water and go upriver until we saw a beaver slide. This is a place where a beaver habitually comes out of the water and up onto the bank. At such a slide we set a trap weighted with a bag of rocks and attached by a six-foot dog chain to a tree or stump above waterline. When caught, the beaver would dive, and held down by the rocks would quickly drown. Beaver, trap, and rocks were easily pulled up by the chain.

All the beaver we caught were taken home at once and skinned — not as most other animals were, so that the pelt made a kind of cylinder, but split up the belly and stretched round, tacked out in a circular shape on a board, just as the French Canadian trappers pegged them out for the Hudson's Bay Company a hundred years ago.

The beaver meat was fed to the dogs, and if there was a surplus it was dried for future use. We girls sometimes ate beaver, finding the meat of two-year-olds very palatable, but Mother and John did not care for it.

During the last few seasons we spent on the Salmon we

changed our habit of trapping beaver only after the ice broke up, and on a few occasions trapped them through the ice, making sets along the river at the various beaver lodges. The water was so clear that the traps were plainly visible, and the beaver could see and avoid them; but with persistence we could catch some. We had a few sets which were as much as a three-day journey to visit and return, and we ran them with the dogs on the last dwindling snow.

On one trip along that line we left Hazel at home with John, and on April 10 Mom, Elsie, and I started out. At the first cabin we left the loads and went on with one team to save time, Elsie and Mom riding the toboggan. The trail was good and the sun bright and warm with spring. Our enthusiasm seemed to overflow into the dogs, and they pulled well until we were halfway to the end of our line. Then they began to slow down. I stepped off the footboard and began to run to make them go faster. By now the sun was melting the snow a little, making the trail hard and slippery. I hadn't run more than a few yards when I slipped and fell. A small, dry, fire-killed spruce about two feet tall hit my cheek and glanced up into my left eye.

"Whoa!" I yelled.

The dogs stopped. "What's the matter?" Mom said. "What are you stopping for?"

I didn't answer. All I could see was black and red. I held my hand over my eye and got to my feet. "Evelyn's hurt!" Elsie said.

They both got out and came back to where I stood, and Mom asked, "What in the world happened?"

I told her, and she took a bandanna out of her pocket and tied it around my head, covering the hurt eye. "Well," she said, "this means we'll have to go back and leave the traps till another time."

But I said, "It isn't much farther to the last of the traps. Get into the toboggan and we'll go on."

"You can't travel with your eye like that."

"I don't travel on my eye," I said. "I can see all I need to with one eye."

"Well," she said, "it's up to you. I think we ought to go back."

But I thought we might as well finish the trip, and not have to come back and do it all over again. Besides, we might get a beaver, and I didn't want to go back skunked.

At the set we were lucky, and got two small beaver. When we got back to the cabin where we were going to spend the night, however, my eye hurt all the time, and when Mom loosened the bandanna and looked at it she said, "That needs attention. I wish we were home. I haven't a thing to work with here."

"We've got time to get home before dark if you want to go," I said. "The dogs aren't very tired."

Mom left it up to me. I told her I wouldn't feel any worse traveling than I did sitting still. By six-thirty we were back in the yard of the home cabin.

John and Hazel helped Elsie put the dogs away while Mom fixed my eye before supper.

I will never forget the next few weeks. Some of the dust from the spruce stick stayed in my eye, and it gathered. Mom put packs of tea leaves on it to draw out the inflammation, but from then until the middle of June I never got away from the pain in that eye, and I never did get so I could see clearly with it again.

But I got along well enough with one eye. I still do.

Our beaver trapping seldom lasted more than two weeks, for by then we would always have caught our limits of ten skins each. And when beaver trapping was over we were almost ready to go. Each year we planted a few lettuce and turnip seeds in our little garden. Then we got the scow into the water, loaded on the winter's fur catch, the camping equipment, and the dogs, hitched on the power boat and the poling boat, and started down the river toward Fort Yukon.

The trip down was no such long-drawn-out voyage as the trip up, for we always started down almost as soon as the river was clear of ice, and had high water all the way. The whole 280 miles seldom took us more than three days. One year we came down the 80 miles of the Salmon and into the Porcupine in four hours. Twenty miles an hour was not too fast for us; by that time we were eager to get to town.

Most years the Salmon River leg took us about five hours. We usually arrived at Pete Nelson's about six or seven in the evening of that first day. One more day's run took us to our customary campsite on Twenty-Mile Bar, which was 20 miles from the mouth of the Porcupine. Before noon of the third day we would be coming around the bend out of the Porcupine into the Yukon, and all eyes would be on the bank a mile up the river where the white buildings and the big tin warehouse of the Northern Commercial store lifted above the little brown log cabins of the town.

2. FORT YUKON

IN JUNE in Fort Yukon the sun shines all night long. I'll never forget those days, usually bright, with the temperature standing at seventy-five or eighty degrees above, the trees in full summer dress, and robins hopping on every fence rail singing their hearts out. The river beach was crowded with boats of all kinds, from poling boats to full-rigged houseboats and barges, except for the one stretch in front of the Northern Commercial store that was kept clear for the landing of the steamboat.

When we arrived in Fort Yukon early in June there was practically nothing in the town to buy. The shelves of the stores were nearly bare, and we always had to plan to get in with enough dog feed and food for ourselves to keep us until the arrival of the first steamboat, which came up the Yukon about the end of the first week in June.

Once the summer service was started, the steamer came every week, but the first trip was the really exciting one, for then the steamer brought large stocks of freight for the three local stores and for residents of the town, and she always stayed from twenty-four to thirty-six hours to unload.

She was an old stern wheeler named the *Yukon*. Five minutes after the first blast of her whistle, every one of the town's five hundred inhabitants would be down at the waterfront, and even the glummest would be wearing a smile. I can see that huge white triple-decker, pushing two barges, chugging slowly up to the landing with a clink of bells, her big wheel splashing, while passengers and crew lining the rail waved hats and handkerchiefs as if they couldn't wait to get ashore and greet people. Even the old cook, in white from head to foot, stood in the doorway of the galley halfway back on the deck and waved a dishtowel.

As the boat eased up to the gravelly beach, the deck hands threw a cable to three or four men on shore who tied it to the "deadman." Then the gangplank was lowered in a lot of confusion and noise, and people swarmed ashore. The plank was hardly clear of them before a dozen or so of the local men crowded on board after the longshoring job. The boat was always in a hurry, and always short of men, so that there was generally work, often the clock around in twelve-hour shifts. Generally the night shift was given to the Indians, and suited them fine, since most of them had just got into town from their rat camps, where they had been hunting muskrats all night and sleeping all day.

In those days the freight was brought off in metal wheelbarrows furnished by the boat. As it was brought off it was put in three big piles, one for each store, and from there it was hauled to the warehouses where it belonged, though this latter job was never completed until two or three days after the steamer left.

On later trips, the steamer would stay in port only a couple of hours, until the very last trip of the year, about September 20. By that time we were always out hunting moose and caribou up the Salmon from our home cabin, or getting the traps ready for the setting out of the lines, but we knew what the last steamer day was like, because we had lived in Fort Yukon. On this trip that brought big supplies to last the town through the winter there would be almost no passengers, often none at all. The nights, instead of being bright and warm and full of excitement and the smell of things growing twenty-four hours a day, would be dark from early afternoon on, and frost would gather on the canvases that were thrown over the big piles of freight on shore. There would be, instead of crowds moving along the beach all through the night, a lonesome watchman patrolling the freight piles, and the *Yukon* would burn her searchlight all night long to prevent stealing, but even so, some of the stuff would walk off.

In the fall it would all be dark and chilly and closing in; in June it was the gayest thing we knew.

Before the steamer ever arrived we would have taken our furs and our kegs of cranberries to one of the stores and sold them to the highest bidder. We would have paid our bills and be sitting around with money in our pockets and nothing to spend it on until the *Yukon* came in and the freight piles were rushed into the warehouses and the shelves filled up in the stores. There was a moving picture show in town, but we seldom went to it, for some reason. And when the movie house was turned into a dance hall, as it regularly was, we didn't go: none of us knew how to dance. But we had our fun, nevertheless. A lot of it came from the passengers and tourists who came in on the *Yukon* and wanted to be shown around.

Fort Yukon was almost entirely a log cabin town, except for the three stores and the Mission and the hospital. Those were the only buildings in the place that were two stories high. The town stretched along the Yukon for about a mile. It had an Indian Service school and the Territorial school. During the one year when my sisters and I went to that Territorial school it had had twelve pupils, only three of us all-white, the others half or quarter Indian. Later, as it got to have two or three times that many pupils, it moved out of the little log cabin where I had gone and into a nice big log house that had been built in the first place as a restaurant.

That wasn't much to show the tourists from the States as they crowded off the steamer with their cameras out, but there was always a crowd along the shore, and we were always glad to show anybody anything he thought he wanted to see. One of the biggest attractions was the Hudson's Bay cemetery half a mile out of town.

In the summer of 1930 the steamer had brought in a Ford car and a truck to one of the local men. The truck was put to work at once hauling freight to the warehouses, and the car became the basis of a profitable business carrying steamboat passengers around to the points of interest, especially to the cemetery. The car owner got most of the trade, but we girls sometimes got a chance to take a bunch on foot.

I remember one time when there were too many for his car, and we had a crowd with us. The road out to the cemetery was narrow and rutted, and it was no easy job to handle the car on it, but the old boy was doing his best despite the ruts and the people walking and blocking the road while they stopped to take pictures. He honked his horn as he worked along, and everyone got out of the road and let him by except one old lady, whom he had brought out himself earlier.

He honked again. She was only a few feet in front of the car, but she didn't move. Exasperation was written all over his face. He slowly eased the car forward until the bumper bumped the most extended part of her. She jumped, lost her balance, and fell. In a second the driver was out helping her up and apologizing, but he hadn't counted on half the wrath he had touched off. She jerked away and faced him, and what she didn't call him hasn't been called.

"Do you know," she told him, "that I've lived in New York City all my life and never been hit by a car? And I have to come out to this one-horse dump and be hit by the only car in the place!"

"I'm very sorry, madam," the driver kept saying. "I honked

three or four times."

She fairly screamed at him. "What are you talking about? Are you afraid to speak? I'll not ride another foot with you!"

The woman next to her said, "She's so hard of hearing she can't hear him at all. I doubt if she even heard him honk."

So we had one more member in our group on the way back to the boat. As she started up the gangplank she said, "I'll never set foot on the streets of this town again!"

She didn't, either. The boat stayed in port for another twenty-four hours, but she never came ashore.

She wasn't alone. Not so many tourists seemed to like our town. Our excursions with them often turned out comically for us but not for the victims. One such was a fifteen-year-old girl who was taking the fresh-air treatment for her ills. She was thin and scrawny and she tried to act very grown up. Also, she didn't have on any more clothes than the law allowed. She wanted to see the Hudson's Bay cemetery.

"You can't go that way," Hazel said. "Go get some clothes on. We'll wait for you."

But no, she would go just like that. She didn't need any advice from small-town teen-agers like us. So she went that way. About halfway to the cemetery, the mosquitoes hit us in full force. Jessie began to slap and stamp. Then she borrowed a shawl from a friend. Her mother said, "Jessie, maybe you'd better go back to the boat."

"I'm going to see the Hudson's Bay cemetery," Jessie said.

"You'd better turn back," I told her. "The farther we go the worse they'll get."

She just turned up her nose. "I'm not a baby. A few mosquitoes can't drive *me* home!"

But as we walked on they multiplied by the hundreds.

Jessie squirmed and stamped and beat at her back with the shawl. Then all at once she screamed, "Mother, I can't stand it!"

She turned and ran for town with a cloud of mosquitoes following her. Someone in the party yelled after her, "Hey, Jessie, I thought you wanted to see the cemetery?"

"Shut up!" Jessie yelled, and kept on going. As far as we could see her she was waving her hands and running. It seemed as if half the mosquitoes around there disappeared with her.

The next time I saw Jessie she had big welts all over her face and arms, but she was fully dressed. She had only one question to ask me. "How can anybody live in this awful place? I hate it!"

Among the tourists we saw on the old *Yukon* was Ernie Pyle, who called himself the "Roving Reporter." He was interviewing people along the Yukon, and one of the families he talked to was ours. Later he wrote a piece, mainly about Mom but partly about our whole family, in the *Reader's Digest*, and worked it into his book *Home Country*. He seemed especially interested when I let it out that I used to write poems on the trip upriver, and set them adrift when I had them done. He told me I ought to keep a diary, and I told him that I had had only one year of school. He didn't seem to think that mattered. He thought I should write down my experiences, and how we felt out on the traplines, because he thought it unusual that four women and a man past seventy should be running a trapline 280 miles from the nearest town.

Ernie Pyle was very friendly and nice. But what he didn't know was that I had been keeping a diary for quite a long time. I generally lost it about as fast as I got a book full but I did spend a lot of evenings in the home cabin writing it down. There were some things that I couldn't say to Hazel or Elsie as we butchered a moose or fed the dogs, times when the trapline seemed like a kind of prison, and I wanted to dream about something else.

When we started up the Salmon for the first time in the summer of 1928, we were deep in debt to John and the stores. A winter's outfit and supplies, especially at first, when we had nothing built up from previous years, cost anywhere from $1600 to $2000 — just about what a year's catch of furs would bring. So for a while we traded last year's debts for this year's furs, and then got ourselves a new debt for the new year.

As time went on we gradually worked the debt down. We never spent a cent we didn't have to, and in buying supplies for the next season we almost always left out butter, jam, candy, dried fruit, everything we could do without. For butter we could substitute moose tallow; for jam and dried fruit we could substitute wild berries. Candy we could do without.

Little by little we got a more or less permanent outfit together, and little by little we whittled down the debt. But in 1937, when Ernie Pyle came through and talked to us about the life we led, we were still not quite out of debt, though we had been out on the trapline for ten years. Hazel was twenty-one, I would be twenty at the end of July, and have my birthday celebration on some gravel bar on the Porcupine or Black River. Elsie, the baby, was seventeen.

We were growing up, or already grown, and we had friends, including boys, among the gang that gathered on the beach every June to welcome us in and gathered again two weeks later to see us off, after the shortest and least satisfying of stays. We were grown women, and it didn't look as if we would ever get far enough ahead to have any kind of life but snowshoeing along some drifted-over trail on the trapline.

1. WINDSTORM

ON JULY 1, 1938, our boats were all loaded, and we were just about to put the dogs on board and shove off when across the Yukon River we saw sand and silt rising in great clouds and sweeping toward us. The muddy water was already forming big white caps. John yelled at us to leave the dogs and come quick, that we had to get the boats into a sheltered place before the wind hit us.

All along the shore for a quarter of a mile we could hear kids and grownups yelling warnings of the wind as they ran to move their boats. Above town, in the slough, they would be protected, but if they were left on the beach the strong south wind could swamp them by the dozens. With everybody else in town, we rushed to start the engines and push

VII. The Big Year

through the first gusts into the shelter of the slough.

The wind blew hard all that night. We took turns watching, two of us on guard every minute in case it got worse. About eight in the morning John told me to run and tell Mom and the girls to get ready, and get the dogs down. The wind had slackened some, and he thought we could get around the corner into the Porcupine, where it would be safer. We were all glad enough to try it. We had been baling all night, and some of the waves had come clear over the side of the scow.

Each of us taking a couple of dogs at a time, we hurried them down to the boats, and in twenty minutes we had them all aboard and were cranking the engines. Then Mom said, "Look across the river. There's another big wind coming."

It seemed as though the little sand islands were rising straight up into the air. Twisters filled the whole air with sand and silt as they came boiling down across the river. In a big hurry we took the dogs off and tied them to the willows and got ready to bail some more.

The wind blew madly all day until about five o'clock, when it slacked off again. Again we locked up the house, loaded the dogs, and cranked the engines. This time it was only a matter of minutes until we got around the windy bend and headed up the Porcupine. Within no time at all the wind had died away and the sky was pure blue. It was so clear and warm that when we stopped for the night about fourteen miles up the river we didn't even pitch a tent, but made our beds on top of the loads in the boats.

There was no darkness. Until long after midnight I lay awake through the night that was like an endless afternoon. The sun dipped almost to the horizon and started to rise again. The air was crisp and cool, and everything was beautiful, but there was a lonesomeness in me that I couldn't overcome. I rolled my head over to look at Elsie, and her eyes were open too.

"Haven't you been asleep yet?" I whispered.

"I can't sleep."

"It's awful pretty, isn't it?" I said.

Elsie lay looking upward. She looked chubby and young and girlish. For long stretches out on the traplines we practically forgot we were girls.

"It's pretty, all right," she said finally, "but it's so darn lonesome, and here we are with another whole year of it ahead of us. I wonder how much longer we'll have to stay on this old trapline!"

So she was feeling about the same way I was. "I don't know," I said. "It can't last forever."

Sometime later we fell asleep. When I heard Hazel starting a fire on the beach, and Mom called to us to get up, the sun was high in the sky again. Pete Nelson was dipping himself a cup of water from the river, and it was another summer day, time to get on with the chores of the trip upriver. We had done it so many times now that it was like second nature: camping on the same bars, fishing the same streams and sloughs with Pete, having the same kinds of boat trouble, snag trouble, water trouble; waiting below the same riffles for higher water, berrying in the same patches, getting soaked by the same rains, eating the same bannocks and dried moose meat and fish and tea, getting flooded out by the same rises, having the same dogfights, being eaten by the same clouds of mosquitoes and gnats, lying on the boats in quiet stretches under the same sleepy sun and being whacked awake by Hazel's poling pole on the gunwale.

Still, even though each year we left Fort Yukon less willingly, and thought more about our friends there, and the things we could do in town, there was always fun on the trip up, and we always managed to invent something new to make things lively.

On this trip I seemed to have a lot of bright ideas about sleeping arrangements. Once in the rain Hazel and I set up the seven-by-seven tent on top of the gas cans in the power boat, so we wouldn't have to slop around on the bar, and we set it low and pulled the walls together underneath to form a floor for our beds. That seemed such a fine arrangement, and we were so wet and cold, that we went to bed right after supper and dozed off happily to the sound of the rain on the gas cans and the tent roof.

But about midnight I woke up and thought the bed was a little cool, and when I moved, the mosquito net was wet around the bottom. My brilliant idea was having results. The tucked-under walls of the tent had let the rain run in under our beds, and the caribou skin we used for a mattress was soaked.

Or there was one night, clear and warm, when we didn't bother to set up the tents at all, but slept on the bar. Elsie and I worked for half an hour picking off the big rocks and leveling places for Mom's and John's beds, but when we thought about doing the same for ourselves we were pretty tired of tossing rocks. "Throw down that caribou skin anywhere you want, and I'll sleep on it just as it is," I told Elsie. "A few rocks couldn't keep me awake tonight."

"Me either," she said. "I could sleep on anything."

But when we limped out the next morning we looked at each other and rubbed our joints. "I guess I'm not as tough as I thought I was," she said.

"I guess I'm not either," I said. "I couldn't seem to get wrapped around the bumps, somehow."

Mom came over. "How was your bed?" I asked.

"Oh, fine," she said. "You did a good job on it."

"It should have been fine," Elsie said. "We took a big enough pile of rocks out of there."

Suddenly she began to laugh, and bent to yank aside the caribou skin we had slept on. We had put it right on top of the pile of rocks we had picked out of Mom's bed.

"I don't see how you girls get any rest at all," Mom said. We thought she had something there.

We left Pete, as usual, thanking God for his house, and

went on and into the Salmon.

That summer we were very short of dog feed, and had to fish every chance we got, and also set rabbit snares. We had forgotten the fish net when we left the home cabin to go to town, and so we had to fish for pike and grayling with hook and line. At a place called William Salmon's Cabin, on the right bank of Salmon River, we were stuck waiting for rain in the hills to raise the water, and dog feed was particularly hard to get. The fishing was bad, a bear kept robbing our rabbit snares. Everywhere we went we carried a .30–06 Springfield in the hope that we would run into him, but all we ever found was his tracks.

One day we were fishing downriver and ran across a trapper's cabin on the bank of a dry slough. The first thing we saw inside was a No. 1 steel snare. We looked at it and wondered if we should take it. It might hold a small bear, though not a big one. From his tracks, our rabbit-robber was small.

"Go ahead," John said. "We'll make it right with John Sam when we see him."

So we took it, feeling rather guilty, and went across the river to where the bear had been working every night. We built a pen of dry willows and put some rabbit cleanings in it for bait, hanging the snare at the entrance and fastening it to a big willow tree.

In the morning when we came around we couldn't see anything at first except that the snare was gone. Then we saw the bear up in the willow. He had been caught around the neck, and had climbed the tree and hanged himself. He made us dog feed for three days, and we returned the snare as good as ever to John Sam's cabin. A few days later we shot a large brown bear that lasted the dogs until the water rose and we could go on.

We went on up the Salmon through a thin fog that hung over the sloughs, past the many beaver houses where beaver swam around and slapped the water with their tails. At one place a moose stood in two-foot grass and watched us as we moved slowly upriver past him. His horns were covered with the soft brown hair called velvet.

Because we didn't want to run the risk of low water again, we traveled all night, and at four o'clock in the morning set up camp at the big bluff two miles below our cabin, from which point we always relayed the supplies home. After a pot of tea and some warmed-over beans and bannocks we crawled into our beds with our clothes on. There was no point in undressing: at seven we'd have to be up and working. After a hard day of packing we could settle down and say, like Pete — if we felt like it — Thank God for our house.

Every fall we liked to set goals for ourselves on the number of pelts of each kind we hoped to catch before the end of the season. That year we had hardly got home before we were promising ourselves that this was going to be the biggest catch we'd ever made. After ten years on the trapline, it was time we had something to show. Thirty wolves, we told each other. Thirty wolves or bust. Our biggest catch up to that time had been twenty-three. Generally we had got fewer than twenty.

"You won't make it," John said. "Not thirty."

"Wait and see," we told him.

2. ROPING A MOOSE

BEFORE THE trapping season began in 1938, John, Elsie and I left the home cabin to be gone twelve days hunting. We had two dogs, my Katy and Elsie's Prince, to line the boat, and we took turns on the trackline with the dogs.

I was going to show Elsie how to pole. She hadn't had much experience at it, so I told her to watch me and she would soon catch on to everything that she needed to know about handling the boat. I should have kept my mouth shut.

I was working my way around a steep bank. The dogs were ahead of me, though I still had hold of the rope, which was stretched out tight by the pull of the boat. All at once I slipped, and the rope kept me going until I lit in two feet of water flat on my stomach. According to Elsie I had one dry spot on me, right between my shoulders. Even John laughed.

Then a little farther on we were going over a swift riffle when I saw that the current was setting in hard against the bow. I yelled to Elsie, on the line with the dogs, "PULL hard!"

They pulled hard, and *snap!* went the trackline. Elsie and the dogs went over in a pile on the bar. We poled ashore and tied the line together and made another try at the riffle and went on. A few miles farther on we had to make a crossing right under the break of a riffle. I said to Elsie, "We'll pole out, keeping the nose close to shallow water, and when we come to the swift shoot, you go on poling. That will make us shoot across fast and hit the bar. But if you don't watch out the boat will swing right back into swift water and we'll have to do it over again, so as soon as we hit the bar

I'll jump out with the rope. You watch and I'll show you just what I mean. All you've got to do is keep on poling."

The shoot was only about twenty feet wide. We came up to it as I planned, and as the current hit the bow, I gave one last push on my pole, then dropped it and reached down for the rope. My hand had just closed on it when the boat hit the bar so hard it threw me clear out of the boat in a heap, with the rope tangled around my feet.

Elsie was killing herself laughing. "I see just how you do it now," she said. "The trick is to get out fast."

I was laughing so hard myself I couldn't move, but just lay there until John yelled, "Are you hurt?"

I shook my head and got up. The knees were torn out of both pants legs and the skin was off both my knees. One elbow was also skinned. I said, "Well, I made a three-point landing and skinned all three points."

We wobbled around laughing ourselves weak, but John yelled, "Go on! We can't sit here all day while you crazy girls laugh."

When I started to untangle the line I found my right thumb was helpless. I had turned it back when I lit. Finally I got the rope straightened out and hoisted the dogs out of the boat and tied them on, but I was limping and laughing at every step.

Elsie said, "I'll take the dogs and you can pole, and then your legs won't hurt so much."

But I said, "Honey Bunch, I couldn't hold that pole on a bet. My thumb's not working."

I lined that bar, and then took the pole to cross. With my right thumb helpless it was hard to hold the pole, but we got along all right until Elsie's pole hit mine and knocked it out of my hands. I grabbed with the good hand and got it again, but as I jerked it up it hit Elsie's and we both dropped them. Each of us made a wild grab, and the boat rocked and heaved. Giggling and snickering, we retrieved them and went on.

As I poled the boat in and coiled up the rope at the head of a bar, I heard a moose bawling across the river in the cotton-woods. Elsie and I wanted to cross and go after the moose quietly, but John said we would walk up the cutbank on our side and look across and see if we could see him. I was pretty sure we wouldn't see him from there, but John was hard to argue with, and I went along, leaving Elsie to keep the dogs quiet in the boat.

When we had gone only a little way, a small moose came out of the woods on our side and started swimming the river. John waited until he had almost made the bar before he shot. It took four shots to bring the moose down. As he dragged himself out into the water a little way and lay there we could see that his back was broken near the hind legs.

"You'd better shoot him again or he'll get out into deep water," I said.

"We can't waste ammunition like that," John said. "He can't get away. We'll cross over and finish him."

So we crossed, and I put the dogs on the trackline and was reaching for my gun when John yelled, "What are you doing? He can't get away. Leave the gun in the boat, and quit fooling around!"

As we came up, the moose pivoted in shallow water, and faced the river. I stopped. John yelled, "Damn it, go on!"

"He'll get out in deep water if we don't kill him."

"Go on, go on!" John said.

The moment we started again the moose started dragging

himself out into the river. I looked back. "Oh, go on!" John shouted. "What in the hell are you waiting for?"

The next thing we knew the moose was swimming. He got over on the cutbank side and got in between two big logs that were rooted in the bank and floating there, and there he stayed.

"That's just what I thought he'd do," I said.

"Oh, shut up!" John said.

We tried crossing the river to chase him out of where he was wedged, but the moose didn't think that way. From the bank we yelled at him and threw cottonwood sticks, but he didn't move.

"Let's get a pole and push him out," John said. "If we can get him started, he'll swim across to the bar."

The dry willow pole I tried to push him with broke on the second or third shove, and I almost went in on top of the moose, who was using the two logs to hold himself in the swift water.

John pondered. "We can't shoot him or he'll go down the river and we'll lose him."

"Maybe if we got a rope around his neck we could shoot him and let him float down and pull him in on the bar," I said.

John jumped at the idea. We got the inch rope out of the boat. "You be the cowboy," Elsie said to me. But I didn't figure that I had got the moose into that pickle, and I had already come close to falling in on top of him once. I let John do it. He tried about six times before he finally threw the rope over the moose's neck. He pulled and pulled, but the moose clung there stubbornly in the fast water between the logs. We all pulled: nothing doing.

Finally John told me to shoot the moose through the head

while he hung on to the line. From up on the crumbling bank I looked at the rope, right under the moose's ears, and I had a feeling that if I shot I might hit the rope. I told John so.

"Oh, hell!" he said in disgust. "Give me the gun and you hold the rope."

He fired and the moose's head dropped into the water and the rope parted, right by his ear.

He started drifting downriver. Elsie and I ran for the boat, smashing through the brush and jumping over logs. We poled out and I got the end of the drag line around a front leg, but we were in a riffle and all we could do was pole for dear life to make the bar. At the lower end we hit the willow bank and I got a rope around a willow to hold the boat and moose from going over the break of the riffle. All the time as we got ashore and started pulling the moose in against the current, John was standing up on the cutbank where he had shot the moose last, calling us all kinds of fools. When we had got our game in where it couldn't get away, we crossed back and got him.

3. SETTING OUT SIDELINES

ONE THING we had got out of ten years on the trapline was a system. We could pretty well know in advance what we would need to do and what we would have to have along to do it. When we started out about November 1 that year to put out the lines, we had things worked out to the last detail, and that meant we had a load on.

Mom was driving four dogs, John four, Elsie five, Hazel and I six each. Elsie, Hazel, and I all had over three hundred pounds apiece on our toboggans, Mother and John about one hundred seventy-five apiece. That was plenty, with only six inches of snow, rough trails, and soft dogs.

On those loads were about twenty loaves of frozen bread, about a hundred frozen doughnuts, thirty pounds of dry beans, half a slab of bacon to cook with them, thirty pounds of sugar, thirty or forty of flour, twenty of edible tallow, six of butter, fifteen or twenty of fresh-frozen cranberries, fifty pounds of frozen "mooseburger" patties, a five-pound can of dried milk, two or three pounds of dried eggs, half a dozen cans of tomatoes, a little macaroni, some cheese, baking powder, and salt. Those were our rations for thirty days.

For dishes we carried a big kettle, two frying pans, two small pots, and a plate, knife, fork, spoon, and cup for each of us. Our bedding consisted of caribou-skin mattresses, feather sleeping robes, and pillows. We always carried a full extra change of clothes in case we got soaked. On that first trip we also took five tents, eight by ten, and sheet-iron stoves to go with them, besides five hundred or more traps of various sizes, a collection of steel snares, and between two hundred and two hundred and fifty pounds of cornmeal and dried fish for dog feed.

Hazel drove the lead team, then came Elsie, then Mother, then me, then John. Elsie could move forward or back to help Mother or Hazel if they hung up on trees or niggerheads, and I could go forward to help Mom or back to help John. All the toboggans, even the lighter ones, were too heavy to be moved very easily by hand; we carried strong dry poles about six feet long and two or three inches through for handspikes to pry them back on to the trail.

First day, eight miles to a little cabin on a hillside, which we fixed up for the winter. Second day, a long hard fifteen miles to the place where we were going to put up the first tent. We were tired, but there was work for all of us. We left the dogs in harness until the tent was up. Hazel cut tent poles while I shoveled away the snow. John untied the leash lines on the toboggans, Mother and Elsie cut spruce boughs for the tent floor. When Hazel and I got the tent up, they broke the boughs into small twigs and covered the floor. I set up the campstove on two green spruce blocks. Hazel brought an armload of wood and started the fire. We spread out the caribou skins, tanned with the hair on, for mattresses, and laid out the sleeping robes on top. Dishes and grub came in from the toboggans, Mom melted snow for water, we girls unhitched all the dogs. While we cut wood John went in and lay down on his bed. Between turns on the saw we bedded down the dogs, and then I went in and cooked dinner while Hazel and Elsie finished splitting the sawed wood. It was moonlight before we were done with our outdoor work and could eat. Then we fed the dogs.

Next day, sidelines to put out. This meant four people and two teams, two people and a team for each sideline. Equipment was an ax each, a big rifle and a .22 for each pair, twenty or more traps, and bait. We took no bedding or food, for we would be back at the tent that night.

If the leader knew the trail, he went ahead. If not, one of us walked ahead cutting and blazing the trail. When we saw a marten track we blazed a tree with two blazes and built a brush house and made a set with bait at the back and the trap in front. Once in a while we made a trail set for wolves or wolverines. If we ran out of traps and saw a lot of fur sign we blazed likely places with three blazes so we could fill them in next time around.

Fourth day, a daylight start and everything going fine until we were about halfway to our next stop, when Hazel's soft dogs began to quit. I gave her Katy to put behind her leader, Punch. Then her female, Bridget, quit, and Elsie traded her leader, Prince, and put Bridget in her own team. Elsie and I kept swapping dogs with Hazel until we had all her dogs except Punch, and she had all the best dogs from our two teams. Elsie and I got along all right because Hazel's dogs would work if they had a team ahead of them.

That night another tent to set up, wood to cut, everything to be got ready, as at the first one. Next day, two of us girls put out sidelines, the girl who stayed behind cut wood with Mom, and John stayed inside and kept the fire burning.

The first day at that tent, Hazel and I put out a sideline. The next day, Elsie and I were supposed to follow a trail that I had not been over since I was eleven years old, the first year we came out to the Salmon. After a good start, we lost it completely. Finally, when I had tried without success to get back on it, I told Elsie to bring the ax from the toboggan.

"What are you going to do?" she asked.

"I'm going to make a trail all your own for you," I said.

We never saw the old trail all day, but we set out twenty-four marten traps and cut eight miles of new trail. By the time we started back it was getting dark. Making the trail, we had wound around the sidehills high up, and crossed the heads of all the little gullies. It seemed now that if we were not going straight up we were going straight down. We would ride a little way down, and then walk a long way up. We had nine dogs in the team, part Elsie's and part mine, and on every downhill stretch they speeded up. If we saw that we were going to hit a small tree we hollered "Whoa!" but it did little good. The tree usually went down and the driver, riding the footboard, usually wound up inside the toboggan on top of the passenger. When we could stop laughing enough to get straightened out, the dogs would be wagging not just their tails but their whole bodies, looking as if they were enjoying it as much as we were. Two especially, Elsie's Pike and my Dick, would look back at the top of each pitch and start jumping at the dogs ahead to get them started galloping.

Once Elsie lost the brake at the top, and the toboggan started down on top of the dogs. "Get out of the way!" we yelled. Dogs jumped left and right, and the toboggan ran down between them. Some of my dogs and some of Elsie's started to fight. The others were all piled up on the other side of the trail. We didn't have a whip, so I yelled, "Straighten them out, Katy!" and Elsie shouted, "Get along, Prince!"

They started, and most of the others followed, leaving only Dan and Dick fighting. As soon as they all got pulling, the two fighters were straightened out and couldn't get at each other. Dick, ahead, would look back and growl, and Dan would dig as hard as he could to catch up with Dick. We were tired and out of wind, and sore from laughing, and we had had two more dogfights by the time we got over the ups and downs of that hillside.

When we reached the flat three miles from camp, Elsie said, "Now maybe we can stop laughing."

"Why?" I said.

The dogs were pulling, eager to get home, across a small lake. I stood up on the back of toboggan, one foot on the back bar and the other on the end of the handlebar, and started riding across. Elsie clapped and yelled till she got the team galloping, but I still stood up. "I'll bet you can't do that over the niggerheads," she said.

"I bet you couldn't either."

"I could for a while."

"So could I."

I stayed on for about fifty yards. There was nothing to hold on to, just two icy poles two inches in diameter to stand on while the toboggan flipped and flapped over the niggerheads. All at once I found myself on my head in the snow between the clumps, about ten feet off the trail.

As I came up blowing, Elsie said, "Can you get out, or shall I pull you out?"

"I'm all right," I said. Then the dogs ran away with her, and she was laughing too hard to stop them. Finally she threw the toboggan against a tree.

I came up and got in. "Let's see if you can do any better," I said. She climbed on the handlebar but as soon as the team started she fell off.

"Terrible," I said.

"You got balanced on the lake before we hit the niggerheads," she said.

"Well, wait till the next lake and you can start there."

She did, and she stayed on about as long as I had before she went on her head in the snow.

We both tried it several more times. At the little lake where the tent was, we both stood on the handlebar and back bar and held hands and rode across the lake that way. Hazel heard all the other dogs barking and came out. "You crazy nuts," she said, "you'll kill yourselves yet."

She told Mom what we had been doing, and got us bawled out. We were not supposed to do that again. But a couple of days later Hazel was out with us and we told her more about what we had been doing coming home that night. So she said, "If you can ride that way for fifty yards, so can I."

The first time she tried it she took a header, close to a little tree, and tore a slit a foot long in her pants leg. The next time her toboggan hit a tree and she went clear over it. Hazel said she was going to stop that nonsense before she killed herself or lost all her clothes. That night she had to sew up her pants, but she didn't tell Mom how she had torn them.

We put up a third tent, and then a fourth, and from the fourth one we again had to set out sidelines. Hazel went with John, Elsie and I went together. They got in from their side-line about three, Elsie and I about six. We had set sixteen traps.

"How far'd you go?" John asked.

"About eight miles," I said.

"And how long were you coming back?"

"Two hours."

"You didn't go any eight miles."

I explained that our dogs traveled fast coming home, but he insisted we couldn't handle the toboggan that fast over the niggerheads. That made us mad, and we made up our minds the next day to stay out until it was good and dark.

We did that. We went ten miles and set twenty-six traps, and we only turned around when it was too dark to see any more. Coming home, we knew that if we broke one mile of short-cut trail we would hit the hard trail that Hazel and John had made the day before; otherwise we would have soft trail and a lot of niggerheads and a longer way back.

I walked ahead of the dogs and we got along fine until we hit the big spruce timber. In there it was as dark as midnight;

we could only see straight up, and then all we could see was stars. I kept to one side of the creek until I saw an opening on my right, when I went out and hit a trail. But after I had looked at it a minute I went back to Elsie and said, "Well, we're back where we started from. We got lost in there."

"This time try crossing the creek when you come to it," Elsie said.

There was no moon, and it took us a long time to find our way, but by crossing the creek we did finally hit Hazel's trail. We got home two hours after dark. When he heard how many traps we had set, John said, "Well, maybe you got far enough for today. You can extend it later."

Elsie and I looked at one another. "If you want that line any longer you'd better take a tent with you and stay overnight," she said.

She was just about right; we never did get in off that sideline in daylight.

When we put the fifth tent out, John said we had to have a caribou. We couldn't be hauling meat way out that far. Our meat supply was getting short anyway, but no amount of hunting in the valleys got us any caribou. They were all up in the white hills.

Before daylight one morning we took sandwiches and a candy bar and started out after them. By ten o'clock we were on top and separating so as to have a better chance for shooting. Hazel and Elsie got around their side a little ahead, and scared up three caribou that ran right in front of me. I shot four times and never hit a hair of them as they leaped across the hill and out of sight like rabbits.

Finally, after a lot of climbing around, we sneaked up on

a bunch over behind some black rocks, and though we were shooting at about two hundred and fifty yards, we finally hit one. So there we were way up on top of the world, a long way from home, with a caribou. We hated the very thought of having to come back next day and climb that hill again after him. Finally Elsie and I took hold of him by the horns and front legs and started pulling him down the steep hill. He came like a sled. When we got him down past the steepest part of the hill we tied a rope on him and all pulled. At the foot of the hill we took the guts out and left him until we could pick him up in the morning, and we had a long long walk under the northern lights to the tent. We had thought we were tough, but that climbing left us stiff and sore.

Thirty wolves, we kept telling ourselves. This is the Big Year. We put out all the traps we had, and cut a lot of new trail. A day or two after the caribou hunt, Hazel and I were putting out a sideline up a long green valley. Almost at the head of it we came upon very big bear tracks, then some smaller ones, then some more big ones. Within a quarter of a mile we found five different sets of bear tracks, all fresh. The dogs sniffed and whined at first, and tried to get past Hazel to run after the bears. But then we came on a sixth bear track, and Hazel said, "I think I could go a little faster if I had my gun in my hand. These things are getting bigger and fresher every minute."

A little farther on her leader stopped and wouldn't go any farther. "Go on, Punch!" I yelled. He just stood there and growled.

Hazel looked back and called, "Come on, Punchie." He moved up to where she was, but when she started to go on, he stepped in front of her and growled. All the dogs were looking the same direction; all were barking quietly, or growling.

Hazel took out her watch and looked at it.

"Is it time to go home?" I asked.

"I think it is!" Hazel said, and we both laughed. The dogs turned around very willingly, and their hair didn't lie down on their backs until we got past the last bear track. What is more, we never went back to that valley to look at our traps until January. A grizzly bear is nothing to play around with at that season, and five or six grizzly bears all at once seemed like a few too many.

Some days later, however, Hazel and I were out again, scouting for a likely-looking patch of marten, and we each had a heavy rifle along. About a mile from camp we found a grizzly track. "Are you real brave today?" Hazel said.

"I sure am," I said.

"Then let's follow this old devil to his den and drag him out dead or alive."

"Let's wait till he's dead," I said. "If we don't wait till *he's* dead before we start dragging, *we* soon will be."

"When we find his den," Hazel said, "you go ahead in, and while he's killing you I'll shoot him."

"No, I'll do the shooting," I said. "You go in and I'll wait till something comes out and if it's brown I'll shoot."

"Then I better not come out head first."

We followed that bear track all day. Just as we were thinking of turning back we saw something coming down the river. We could just see a moving back over a drift. We ducked down quick. But after a minute I said, "That didn't look like a bear to me." We raised up again, and the bear had turned into a wolverine that was now heading up a very steep bank near the river's edge. Hazel took a shot at him and I saw the bullet kick up snow just below him. She shot again and he rolled up in a ball and rolled all the way down the hill. As we walked over to the river we kept our eyes out for him, but when we saw him he was moving, and he was out of sight in the next jump. Until dark we followed his bloody trail. He was shot through the middle, and though he tried several times to climb a tree, he couldn't make it.

We didn't get the wolverine, but we got a long way from camp. As for the bear track, it went on up the river.

The next day we put out a sideline. Hazel said, "If we can't catch a wolverine or a bear, maybe we can catch some marten."

"Or thirty wolves," I said.

We put out a good long line and moved on, up what we called Windy Valley. Here we set up our last tent, and from it Elsie and I put out one sideline, and Hazel and John put out another. Hazel and John set out only eight traps, but Elsie and I were after a big catch, and we could get around a little better than John could. We put out twenty-five. Then we went on over the hills to the head of Wind Creek where we had an out-cabin.

That cabin was all frosty, and its roof dripped for a couple of hours after we got the fire started, but we were glad enough not to have to put up a tent. For two days Mom and Elsie cut wood while Hazel and I put out two sidelines, and then we cut over the hills to the second tent, the one by the lake where Elsie and I had tried being toboggan acrobats. We took a quick run over Elsie's sideline and got three marten before we started for home.

4. GOAL ACHIEVED

THE SPRING before, Bill O'Brien's cabin had gone into the river. When he came up with us he had said he was going to move across the Canadian line, where his trapline was, so that we needn't bother to come by to see how things were with him. Usually we managed once or twice a winter to drop in on Bill, for he was old and alone, and even if we all hadn't liked his company we would have wanted to see how he was doing.

On our way home from putting out our lines, we stopped at the place where his lowest cabin had been. There was a little grub in the cache, and an almost snowed-out toboggan trail that we could not follow because it ran through a slough where there had been an overflow.

"It looks as if he only comes down here for supplies off the cache, and is living over on the Canadian side as he said he would," John said. That meant he was all right. On the Canadian side he would be looked in on by the Mounties two or three times during the winter.

We set out all the traps we had on the way home, and Hazel and Mom left the rest of us to do that while they ran over some of the lines we had put out earlier. Thirty wolves! we kept telling ourselves. We didn't want to miss any chances.

John and Elsie and I finished putting out the traps and started for the trapline cabin. The sky was dull gray, and it looked as if it might snow that night. It was the end of November, and twenty below, and as we thought about the little seven-by-eight cabin, and how much nicer it would be in the big home cabin, especially if Mom and Hazel had got there first and warmed things up, we decided that we would go on home, even if it meant running late.

In the gloomy dusk I drove my team into the home-cabin yard. The moon was just a blur behind the clouds, and snow was beginning to fall. As I passed the little garden spot I saw a number of big holes punched in the snow. I thought that maybe a moose had been through the yard, or that Hazel might have punched them trying to fool us; she was always trying that kind of trick. But I looked across at the cabin and there wasn't a light in the window. Everything was dark. I had my face fixed for warmth and light and hot food, and I was disappointed. When my leader started to go into the shed I yelled at him, "Happy!"

With a growling bark he jumped to the left and started out on the trail to Hazel's trapline. I had to shout at him twice before he stopped. He continued to growl and bark, and his hackles were up stiff.

I felt my own hackles go up. The tall spruce timber behind the cabin was dark; the dark shadows among the snowy lighter openings could have been moose, wolves, anything. I watched for any of them to move, but everything was still. Flakes of snow fell silently and brushed my face.

By now all the dogs were growling softly and all were staring toward the house. Without taking my eye off the dark cabin I reached and loosened the ropes that held my Krag on top of the load.

I was looking in the dark window, which was just opposite the other window at the back of the cabin. I could look right through the black house and out into the snowy, blurred gloom beyond. And then it seemed to me that something black filled most of the opening of the window, and that I could see only the smallest frame of lightness around it.

My muscles tightened as stiff as wire; I held my breath while I stared. Could it be a bag of clothing or straw that Hazel or Mom had hung there? Or could my eyes be blurred with dark and snow, and seeing only shadows? Or could it be something else?

Elsie drove up behind me and stopped. I heard her say, "What's the matter? What are you and your crazy dogs staring at?"

"Look," I said. "From here, where I am." My voice sounded strange even to myself. I stepped aside so she could look, and as I moved it seemed to me that the object in the window dropped straight down.

"What was that?" I said.

Elsie said uncertainly, "It was your reflection, I think. It looked like it had ears, but it moved when you did."

John called from behind us, "Oh, go on in and start a fire. There can't be anything in there."

But I had no desire to go into the house right then. Except for our voices, half whispering, and the growling and woofing of the dogs, the place was as quiet as death. I felt like someone about to enter a haunted house at midnight. Elsie walked across toward the house and I half lifted my rifle, expecting anything. She disappeared around the corner of the shed. A moment later she came running back.

"There *is* something in there! It sounded like somebody walking across the floor with hobnailed boots on!"

"Get your gun ready," John said, and started digging in his pocket for a box of matches.

We all stepped carefully into the shed. As we entered John lit a match, and in the quick flare of light we saw that the door to the cabin was wide open and that everything in the shed had been knocked down. The place smelled like an old stable. Just as the match went out I pulled the door shut, and instantly some pots and pans fell inside with a loud clatter.

By the light of some more matches we splintered a stick of wood and poured gasoline over it to make a torch. I cocked the rifle and knelt down on one knee while John held the torch above and behind me. Then Elsie pushed open the door again.

I looked in the flickering torchlight across a floor littered with pots and pans. The bunk bed was directly opposite me, at the far end of the room, and in the bed sat a grizzly bear. He looked at me as I took aim, and I knew that if I didn't hit him right we would have plenty of trouble on our hands.

I shot. Fire streaked from the gun with a light that dazzled me. When I could see again, the bear lay motionless on the bed. As much by luck as anything else, I had hit him where I wanted to.

Elsie and I ran in and rolled him off the bed. As he thumped on the floor we jumped back for fear he might come back to life again, but he didn't.

John lit the coal-oil lamp and put the torch in the heater to start a fire, and Elsie and I pulled the blood-soaked bedding off and threw it outside to freeze until we could get around to washing it.

"What a mess I made," I said, "killing that thing on the bed."

Elsie laughed. "Why didn't you ask him to get down before you shot?"

"I didn't think of it," I said. "Come on, let's drag him out of here."

We put the dogs away and unloaded the toboggans and set up housekeeping, but the smell of bear was with us for a long time. Mom and Hazel got back just in time to clean up the last of the wreckage. That was once, Mom said, when it had really paid them to be late.

One bearskin. But what we wanted was marten, mink, ermine, wolverines, fox, especially wolves. We had our hearts set on that goal of thirty. For a long time we didn't think we were even going to come close. And then luck turned our way and the caribou herd came through.

They came streaming up from the south the way they had on my first trip out on the lines with John. The timber was moving with them, the flats were thicketed with their horns, the snow was pawed up everywhere, you couldn't look in any direction without seeing the dark shapes and the big antlers moving northward. And right into that northward migration came a south-moving herd just as big, and behind and around and in front of both herds were the wolves.

There were wolves everywhere. We met them on the trails, saw them running on the flats and the hills. We got ready to find our traps and snares full of them, but nothing happened. All along our traplines the packs killed hundreds of caribou, so many that they wouldn't look at any bait we put out.

In the midst of all that, it didn't seem too much to want to catch thirty, and yet more and more caribou kept streaming past, and more and more wolves were on their fringes, and we didn't catch a thing.

Then, just as suddenly as they had started coming past, the caribou were gone. We saw fresh tracks heading north and fresh tracks heading south, but no more caribou. The two big herds, one going each way, must have met and passed right on our trapline. And when they disappeared they left the poor wolves completely bewildered about which way to go. I suppose that many followed on the trail of each herd, but hundreds of them were left behind right where we wanted them.

With no caribou to kill, they soon got hungry. They ate up all the old killings and cleaned up the skin and bones, and finally they came to our bait and we began to catch them. Then we had something else to grumble about, for if one got caught in a trap, at least half the time other wolves would eat him before we got there. Time after time we found our sets with a gnawed leg between the jaws, and a scattering of blood and fur on the snow, and we reset them and caught more, and half of them were eaten. But in spite of the losses we began to accumulate quite a pile of big black or gray wolf carcasses on the cache, and by the time the big flurry of the caribou-wolf migration was over we had hit our thirty.

Thirty? we said. Why not forty? If we were going to be stuck on an old trapline we might as well make it worth while.

We had not made our forty when the season closed, but we had one outside chance, for Hazel had a permit to continue snaring wolves after the end of the trapping season. She and Elsie left out all the wolf snares when they picked up their traps. At each camp they left the tents, stoves, and traps to be hauled in later. On about March 25 they were in camp on the edge of a lake, and left the dogs on the trail and their rifles in the toboggan while they went to look at the snares.

As they walked, Elsie saw something dark in the distance.

"What's that over there?" she asked Hazel.

"Oh, come on!" Hazel said, imitating John. "If it's any-thing, it's a bear."

But Elsie said, "I'm not going any farther till you take a look."

"All right, just to please you," Hazel said. "Where is it?" She took one look where Elsie pointed and said, "Gosh, it *is* a bear, and a darn big one. We'll head for the toboggan and get our guns."

They started, and so did the bear, straight toward them. They had about as far to go to the toboggan as he did to reach them, but they were running in the caribou trails and their steps were so short they couldn't make much speed.

"Hurry, Hazel, he's coming!" Elsie yelled. The dogs jumped to their feet and started to bark. Then the bear stopped, listened a minute, and walked quietly back to the caribou he had been eating. They got their guns and went back and shot him there. That was our second grizzly skin that winter — this one with a nose-to-tail measurement of nine feet and an armspread of eleven.

Two bearskins. And thirty-eight wolves. We weren't going to make our forty. On about April 1 we left home for the last time to haul in all the tents, stoves, and traps from the girls' lines. We would have to move fast, for the creeks might break up before we got back.

The trail was good to the first tent, and we arrived early. Hazel said, "Let's go over to the lake. I lost a wolf snare there last winter and there was so much snow I couldn't hunt it up. Now that the snow is settled maybe we can find which way it went."

We all took our rifles, just in case we met any more bears,

and started off on snowshoes. We had hunted without any result for twenty minutes or so, and were sitting on hummocks of grass resting, when I noticed a black spot across the lake, a good half mile away. I thought it might be a muskrat house, but Hazel said there were no rats in this lake. It didn't look like a bear. "Let's go over," Elsie said.

The closer it got the more mysterious it looked. It looked like some sort of fur. "I'll bet it's your snare with a wolf in it," I said. We broke into a run, and as we got close we all yelled at the same time, "A wolf! A black one!"

That made us thirty-nine. On the way back to camp Hazel and I traded off, one carrying the wolf while the other carried two rifles. We were all agreed we just *had* to get one more to make our forty, but there were only a few snares still out.

The next day we went over the whole line as fast as we could, and there was not a wolf in any of the snares until the last one. That had a big gray fellow, and we had our forty.

During the middle of the day the snow thawed so much that we couldn't travel. We had to get up and move about two in the morning, and could travel only until about noon. By four o'clock in the afternoon we would be in camp and in bed. Already the snow was nearly gone from the south-facing slopes of the hills. Since much of our traveling was northward, this meant that on a lot of the hills we had to haul the toboggans over bare ground, which was four times as hard on the dogs and on us as pulling them on snow. Even at four in the afternoon, we were not unwilling to get to bed.

The dogs were very tired as we came to a long bare hill. Hazel's dogs quit on it, refusing to pull the load over the grassy niggerheads, and after trying to start them again she had to give up. They were just too tired to go on without a rest. And yet if we didn't get along we might find that the ice on Wind Creek had gone out and we would be stranded on the wrong side.

Elsie and I wanted to camp, Hazel wanted to go on. A duck flying over the trail warned us that the breakup was nearly on us, for whenever you see ducks flying north spring is close. But there was little Hazel could do, so we camped. We had only two sleeping robes with us, one of them a light one. At two in the afternoon, with the sun shining on us, it was warm. I told Hazel to take the feather robe, and Elsie the light robe and a caribou skin, and I would roll up in a tent.

About seven that evening I woke up shivering. The sun had set and a strong cold wind was blowing. No matter how I cuddled down in my tent I couldn't get warm. Elsie was stirring, too, but Hazel snored on in her comfortable nest of feathers. Finally I stuck my head out and said to Elsie, "Are you cold, Honey Bunch?"

"You're darn right," she said. "Are you?"

"I'm darn near frozen."

Hazel opened her eyes and said, "What's the matter, are you poor little kids cold? You must be too cold-blooded to keep warm. I'm warm as toast."

We offered to trade, but she felt fine where she was. After a while she suggested that we put all three beds together, and then we were warmer. At two in the morning we were up and on our way, without even a cup of tea to drink because in the niggerheads it was dangerous to start a fire.

On the thawing trail and the half-bare slopes we worked

very hard, for several days, living on bread and tea and tough caribou tongue. Each morning we started by two or two-thirty, when the frost was still heavy on the grass and the air was cold. It seemed much colder than in the winter, somehow. Maybe because we wanted it to be spring. We warmed up climbing the hills on the sunny side, and got chilled walking down the shady side, and all the time Hazel kept after us to hurry because if we didn't we would find the ice in Wind Creek out.

At five one morning we reached the little cabin only six miles from home, all downgrade. Hazel wouldn't let us rest more than a minute. I said, "I wish you'd forget that darn creek for about ten minutes. If it's going out, we can't stop it by talking about it all the time. Look at the fun we'd have building a raft or hopping across the ice pans like Little Eva."

"You nut," Hazel said, "you know perfectly well that if that ice moves, we won't get across at all."

"That would be all right with me," Elsie said. "We've got plenty of grub. If we can't get across we won't have to work all spring."

Hazel just looked disgusted.

At six-thirty we reached Wind Creek, and sure enough the creek was running a flood of water. But as we walked to the edge we could see that the ice was still holding under the brown surface stream, though the water was two feet deep on top of it.

"We can't cross that," Hazel said. "The dogs would be swimming, and they can't pull that way."

"Let's put them all in one team," I suggested. "Then the leaders would be across before the toboggans started."

"All right," Hazel said. "We could tie the three toboggans together so they won't tip over if the current hits them."

We started the leaders into the water about fifty feet above the trail to allow for the current carrying them downstream as they crossed. They plunged right in and swam across. When we had three on the far shore we stopped them and hooked the tugs onto the toboggans. "All right, boys," we said.

The toboggans hit the water and the spray flew. The creek was eighteen dogs wide. When we were two thirds of the way across, each in her splashing toboggan, we all hollered "Whoa!" but the dogs had such a hurry on that they didn't stop until they pulled us into the mudbank. Using all the dogs in one team, we got the toboggans up the bank one at a time and started on the last leg home.

We were feeling really good. It was spring, and the season was practically over, and the trip down to Fort Yukon seemed in sight, though it was still two months away. What was left was cleanup work, skinning, storing, drying meat, getting our limit of beaver. We were always sure of doing that without trouble, and we could already count it in the season's catch.

It was the biggest catch we had ever made. We had more than sixty marten, thirty ermine, ten mink, thirteen fox, four wolverines, two grizzly bears. We would have fifty beaver. And we had, not the thirty wolves we had set as our goal, but forty, and two coyotes besides. If we could have saved all we had trapped the catch would have been tremendous, because Hazel and Elsie caught forty wolves that winter and saved only twenty-three of them, and I caught thirty and saved only seventeen.

Even so, we were pretty sure it was going to be the biggest wolf catch ever brought into Fort Yukon.

It was.

THAT YEAR it seemed as if we had no time at all in Fort Yukon before we were loading up the boats again. Our catch had brought us in $2900, almost a thousand dollars better than we usually did, and we were out of debt at last. And yet we all felt sulky and somehow cheated and dissatisfied. We had worked very hard to make a big goal, and had done it. But when we had it done, what was it? Five people working like dogs through a whole year to make less than three thousand dollars — less than six hundred dollars apiece. And as soon as we got it made it went back into the stores for a new outfit and supplies, and it was all to do again.

Not only that, but all three of us girls had friends in Fort Yukon, people our own age, including boys. It was hard to turn around and leave them after only two weeks, and beat around the windy point and into the Porcupine and start that old slow laborious voyage up toward the Salmon again. We thought we had had about enough fishing, hunting, trapping, and sleeping in tents and out-cabins to last us for a while. All

VIII. The Breakup

of us would have stayed in Fort Yukon at the drop of a hat, but there wasn't any way we could. Even with the big catch, we were barely even after eleven years. A few more big catches would put us far enough ahead so that we could sell the line and move to town, maybe even to Fairbanks. Mom had half promised that, if we could ever get a real stake.

We had never been to Fairbanks, any one of us. None of us had even seen a town bigger than Fort Yukon, and none of us could remember any other town at all. But Fairbanks seemed closer, since air service had got common. It was still a million miles off, but the plane came over in an hour and fifteen minutes. Though it didn't really seem possible that we could ever get so far, we told ourselves it was and tried to believe it. And we even had a feeling of being much more in touch with civilization out on the Salmon, because Mom had arranged with Jim Dodson, the town's first brush pilot, to drop us a load of supplies in December.

I wrote a lot of poems and set them adrift down the Porcupine and the Black that summer of 1939. I filled up a lot of diaries, all of which I lost later. And on quiet stretches when the roar of the Kermath motor and the slap and ripple of the water were the only noises, and the sun poured down on the boats and the green shores went by, bar and cutbank, spruce and cottonwood, alder and rosebush and grassy slough, all three of us girls were likely to be a long way away, just imagining things.

This summer, too, Bill O'Brien wasn't with us. He hadn't showed up in Fort Yukon at all, and we didn't know whether he had moved way over on to the Canadian side or had had some kind of accident. It didn't seem likely that he would move clear out, because there were no posts anywhere near on the Canadian side, and the only logical way out from his trapline was down the Salmon and the Porcupine.

It didn't seem quite the same without Bill, and his firebug habits, and his slow talk. When we left Pete at his cabin, thanking God for his house, he seemed like a lonesome old man, a little queer from living alone too much. And we had not been very long at the home cabin before we got word of Bill. A search party had found him in a tent, just across the river from the lowest cabin where we had tried to visit him in the winter and found only the half-snowed-out toboggan trail and the cache with a little food. Bill hadn't moved across as he had said he was going to, but had set up a tent across the river. Sometime during the winter he broke his leg. When the search party found his body they found no firewood and no food in the tent. Bill had shot himself in the head with his rifle. It all might have happened about the time we went through and saw his tracks and thought he was away on across the boundary. If we had crossed the river we might have found him before his food and wood gave out.

Bill's death seemed to set the whole year off wrong. We had tried to get ourselves excited about making another big catch this year and, with one big effort, getting far enough ahead to quit, but right from the beginning things went bad. The hunting was very poor: we went out time after time, but we didn't get more than half the meat we needed. To make it worse, John was getting old, and the older he got the crankier he got. He still thought of himself as the boss — after all, he had rescued us when we were in a bad hole, and the trapline was really his, and he had loaned us the money to get an outfit together. But he was getting weak, and his weakness made him mad, and he was harder to please than he had been when he could do more than his full share of the work himself.

Not only was the hunting bad, but we had to build a new cabin twelve miles up Stony Fork, for the old one was about ready to fall down. The very thought of putting up a new cabin, looking as far ahead on that trapline as a new cabin would last, rubbed us the wrong way. The old cabin was damp and cold, and we hadn't brought as much bedding as we could have used, so that we slept cold while we were building the new one. We were short of dog feed, and had to stop work to fish for grayling. Once while we were fishing for grayling we heard moose fighting across the river. At least I thought it was moose. As I stood listening with my hook dangling a foot above the water, a big grayling jumped and took it and I almost jumped out of my skin.

I threw the fish up on the bank. John said, "Listen a minute. I do hear a moose somewhere."

We all stood facing across the river, where the noise had come from. In a minute there came the clash of horns and a thud, and then the crashing of brush. Hazel and I put down our fishpoles and picked up our guns. We didn't want to get caught in the middle of any moose fight in the dark.

"I think we'd better go home," Hazel said. "It's too dark to shoot."

"Never mind them," John said. "They're across the river. We've got to get dog feed."

The vague sounds went on, clash and tap of horns, smashing of brush. "They must be really fighting," Hazel said. She had never been run over by a charging bull moose as I had that time with John on the trail, but she didn't have any more desire than I did to tangle with one in the dark.

A stick broke behind me. I whirled around and looked: nothing but dark woods.

"You've sure got 'em," John said. "What's the matter with you, anyway?"

We went on fishing, watching across the river where the sounds of fighting calmed down and then started again. Again I thought I heard a stick crack behind me, but I wasn't going to whirl around again and get laughed at.

The dogs were sniffing and looking all around. Then all at once the air was full of the smell of moose.

"Darn it, I can even *smell* them, can't you?" I said.

There was a blowing snort right behind us. We all wheeled at once, automatically throwing shells into the chambers of our guns. In a little opening not more than fifty feet away stood a big bull moose silhouetted against the lighter sky, and in the split second when we saw him he dropped his head for the charge.

John shot without taking time to aim. The fire streaked in an orange line almost to the moose. For a moment we couldn't see, but right along with the roar of the gun we heard the sharp click as the bullet glanced off the moose's horns. There was a heavy smashing of brush, and John fired again at the noise, to make sure the bull wouldn't come back. "Get the lines off your poles," he said to us. "We've got enough fish for tonight. Let's get back to camp and get something to eat."

As we bent over our poles, Hazel said to me, "He sure got hungry quick when that moose came around, didn't he?"

With the luck we had had the year before, we might have got the moose, and things might have started to go better. But we didn't get him, and we didn't get any others. We only had two moose for the whole winter. The meat situation was so bad that in late September, after it was too late to go hunting in the boat, we girls each took one of our dogs on a six-foot leash and used them to scent out moose along the several dry sloughs up on Stony Fork.

When Hazel and I, who were hunting together, came to a big U bend of the river, just above the head of a slough, I told her to go around the bend and watch for anything I might scare out as I went straight through. "Stay out on the bar," I said. "Maybe I can root something out of here."

I started through the willows, very thick near the river but thinning and mixed with spruce trees farther back. About halfway through the U bend my dog pulled at his rope and sniffed and looked off to the left. He couldn't have smelled anything, because he was looking downwind; he must have heard or seen something. Thinking it might have been Hazel on the bar, I stopped and looked carefully, but the bar was far away and I saw no sign of her or anything else.

Then a bull moose stepped out of the willows, and before I could move disappeared behind the low branches of a big spruce. He didn't even see us. Happy whined low and tugged at his rope, and I whispered, "Keep still, Happy." Very carefully I threw a cartridge into the chamber of the .30–.40 Krag.

I could no longer see the moose behind the tree, but by staring hard I made out the shadow of his front half through the branches. Raising the gun slowly and quietly, I fired. Right after the report a voice from behind the tree said, "What the hell are you shooting at?" and Hazel stepped out with one hand in front of her face, to ward off the branches, and her dog at her heels.

I was cold all over with the thought that I had shot her, but when I got my voice and asked her if she was hit she said no. "I thought I was shooting at a moose," I said. "I'd have sworn I saw him walk right behind there."

Then three shots rang out in the woods to our right. "Maybe you *did* see a moose," Hazel said. "Maybe that's what Elsie and John are shooting at now."

"Why on earth did you come in here?" I said, still shaky. "You were supposed to stay out on the bar."

She said her dog had acted as if he smelled a moose in the brush. So we went back into the brush and looked, and about as far away again as the spruce Hazel had been under when I shot, we found a set of big moose tracks. He had stopped behind a second tree right in line with the one Hazel had been under, and then had started running, apparently, when I shot. We followed his tracks to where they went straight into the river across a large gravel bar. If Hazel had stayed where she belonged she would have gotten him easily, and I wouldn't have come close to shooting a hole through her.

John and Elsie had shot at another moose that had been scared out of the thick brush. With the luck that seemed incurable that year, they had both missed. We went back to the cabin with frazzled nerves and no meat.

That was the way the whole season of 1939 went. Bad fishing and bad hunting led right into bad trapping. The winter was hard and the fur was scarce. My Katy, who had been my leader for eight years, was dead. John was older and less able to work his share, but he wouldn't change and he wouldn't move, and Mom was afraid to leave the trapline until she got a stake together. Besides, she felt obligated to

John, and he was too old to run his line alone. Something like what happened to Bill might happen to him.

The winter seemed to last for years, and the spring was nearly as long. We could hardly wait to get our little catch of pelts in to Fort Yukon and see the big river again and the brown log cabins strung along its bank, and the two-story Mission and hospital, and the stores and the big tin warehouses, and the *Yukon* puffing and churning and clinking up to the landing with the passengers waving and the crowd yelling on shore. And we had a pretty good notion that some of the boys we knew would be keeping an eye out along the waterfront, looking for our scow and power boat and poling boat to come around the point into the Yukon.

I came downriver that spring with more excitement than anybody else, because during the middle of the winter sometime, when we were all so sick of the hard work and hard food and bad luck of the trapline that we were ready to do almost anything to get out, I had sent a letter downriver with a trapper who passed through. It was written to my boy friend in Fort Yukon, whom I had known for one week, and it said that if he would meet me in Fort Yukon when we came out in June, I would marry him.

Believe me, I was watching the riverbank when we came in. There was a crowd of Indians and trappers and townspeople out to greet us, as usual, but the face I was looking for wasn't there. He hadn't come to town yet. The *Yukon* came, and the spring passengers came down the gangplank, and the trappers came in from their ratting camps and from their far traplines, but he didn't come. I felt as if my letter was like one of the poems I wrote and then set adrift on the Porcupine or the Black, and I kicked myself for depending so much on his answer. I even found it hard to remember what he looked like. I wondered if he had ever existed. A week, even a week of making up for all the lonesome year, and in the Alaskan summer when the sun shines all day and all night, is a pretty small stretch of time to hitch your life on.

The time came for us to pack up, and still he didn't come. And so for the twelfth time we got the dogs aboard and hitched on Pete Nelson's boat and pushed off. When I thought of the long year ahead, and of the years beyond this one, I was ready to jump overboard or bang my head against the gunwale.

Nineteen-forty started just the way 1939 had. We had very poor luck hunting, and by the time the season was over our spirits were away down below zero. I remember one evening when I was about as low as I could get, and the other girls the same, and we took a .22 and a .30–06 and walked out to Wind Creek, not because we expected to get anything but because an evening walk was one way to try to lose the blues.

We were walking through a carpet of low-bush cranberry bushes, not paying much attention to where we put our feet. "Hey!" Elsie said finally. "Hey, don't walk right through the middle of the patch. John says it kills the bushes so there won't be any berries next year."

"Next year!" Hazel said. "Next year. That's all we ever hear. Next year we'll get a good catch. Next year we'll go to Fairbanks. I'm sick of next year."

So was I sick of next year — or last year, for that matter. I said, "Do you kids realize that we're all past twenty years old, and that we've been out here twelve years and we're still waiting for that big fur catch so we can leave? If we don't do something on our own and stop waiting for John to make up his mind to move, we'll be here the rest of our lives."

"I'm twenty-four," Hazel said.

"And still waiting for Mom and John to tell you what to do," Elsie said.

"We'd better wake up and do something ourselves," I said. "The first thing we know we'll be a bunch of old maids."

"Sure," Elsie said. "That's right. But what can we do about it? If one of us leaves, the other two will have all the work to do and they'll *never* get out."

"He doesn't even take the boats to town any more," Hazel said.

I was fed clear up. "Forget about the boats. They can rot on the bank for all I care. I'm twenty-three years old and this will be my last year on Salmon River or else . . ."

Out there in a cranberry patch on Wind River we made an agreement. Next spring we would make a mass runaway. That would make Mom and John sell the trapline and move to town, where they had plenty of friends and would make out doing something. Each of us girls would go her own way, and if any one of the three failed to carry out the plan to run away, it was her own choice and the others would go without her.

We kept the plan to ourselves all that winter, talking about it when we were alone, and adding to the things we were going to do when we got away. But I was the one who was surest of what she wanted to do, because during the winter a letter came in with the airdrop of supplies. The boy I had been looking for during the quick two weeks in Fort Yukon had finally got my letter in July, a couple of weeks after we had left for the year. His views about getting married matched mine, and I knew right where I was going to go when we ran away.

In the end, I was the only one who ran. And I couldn't wait until spring. I went out overland with a dogteam, and was married in Fort Yukon on February 28, 1941.

Though the other girls backed out at the last minute, my leaving started the breakup. Elsie pulled out the next year, made her way over to Fairbanks and worked for Pan American Airways for a while, and the next year married a coal miner from Anchorage. With only Hazel left to do the hard work of the trapline, John finally decided that they would have to give it up, and the family moved into Fort Yukon where Mom started a little bakery.

But what makes all this breakup a little comical is that both Hazel and I married trappers. I had hardly got out of the trapline on the Salmon and got married before I was trapping again, and I trapped with my husband for another nine years, adding to the usual chores the work of raising a family. Four of my five children were born, as I was born, on snowshoes. It would not surprise me at all if some of them, at least, spent most of their lives wrestling loaded toboggans out from between the niggerheads, lighting fires in the icy stoves of snowed-in cabins, making camp in the cold dark in lonesome tents away out in the timber with the northern lights pulsing from horizon to horizon and the wolves howling far away. They will never get rich, but they could do worse. I think that when my son is twelve I will give him for a birthday present my old .30–.40 Krag.